Praise for *Love Y*

'Rita Clifton, as anyone who has ever heard her speak knows, is warm, witty, wise and wonderfully inspiring, and her new book is all of those things too. Reading this book makes you feel like you are in the room with her, with Rita as your own personal mentor as you navigate your life and career. Her advice to people going to speak in public at a gathering of any size is "show up as a human" and nowhere is Rita more human than in this book.' PROFESSOR HEATHER MCGREGOR, CBE (MRS MONEYPENNY), EXECUTIVE DEAN, EDINBURGH BUSINESS SCHOOL, HERIOT-WATT UNIVERSITY

'Finally – someone tackling the imposter syndrome head-on! Enough talking about the fact we have it – at last a book that actually deals with it! If I could have her beside me throughout my own business journey I would. Relatable, funny, down to earth and a woman who's been there, done it and knows what she is talking about. A must-read for every woman across the country.' HOLLY TUCKER MBE, FOUNDER, NOTONTHEHIGHSTREET.COM

'*Love Your Imposter* is a brilliant book and it couldn't have come a better time. We are seeing a human revolution where professional and personal boundaries are blurred, especially for women. This book gives us inspirational yet practical tips on how to navigate this new world. Rita Clifton writes with refreshing honesty about her career and beginnings and explores concepts such as strength in vulnerability, communication and ways we can all be more empathic to ourselves. I loved it!' BELINDA PARMAR OBE, THE EMPATHY BUSINESS

'Rita Clifton has always been a great champion for helping people be their best selves, professionally and personally, and this book helps that cause in a fabulously human way. She is funny, insightful, practical and inspiring.' NICOLA MENDELSOHN CBE, VP EMEA, FACEBOOK

'Most people have felt like an imposter at some point in their career but it takes a modern, twenty-first-century leader like Rita Clifton to put it into a book and have you embrace this emotion of vulnerability.' KANYA KING CBE, FOUNDER OF MOBO AWARDS

'Do you have a voice in your head telling you you're not good enough? Yes? Join the Imposter Syndrome Club! Women's inequality in the workplace is costing the economy trillions of pounds a year. Much could be solved by replacing that voice with the voice of Rita Clifton instead. This jargon-busting business icon and brand guru will get inside your brain and give you the tools you need to get to the top and, most importantly, know you deserve to be there.' KATHRYN PARSONS MBE, CEO AND CO-FOUNDER, DECODED

'A warm, wise and wonderful leadership manual, full of fun and humanity.' DAME CILLA SNOWBALL CBE, CHAIR, WOMEN'S BUSINESS COUNCIL, AND GOVERNOR OF WELLCOME TRUST

Love your imposter

Be your best self, flaws and all

Rita Clifton

KoganPage

First published in Great Britain and the United States in 2020 by Kogan Page Limited

2nd Floor, 45 Gee Street
London
EC1V 3RS
United Kingdom

122 W 27th St, 10th Floor
New York, NY 10001
USA

4737/23 Ansari Road
Daryaganj
New Delhi 110002
India

www.koganpage.com

Kogan Page books are printed on paper from sustainable forests.

© Rita Clifton, 2020

The right of Rita Clifton to be identified as the author of this work has been asserted by her in accordance with the Copyright, Designs and Patents Act 1988.

ISBNs

Hardback   978 1 78966 703 5
Paperback   978 1 78966 700 4
Ebook   978 1 78966 701 1

British Library Cataloguing-in-Publication Data

A CIP record for this book is available from the British Library.

Library of Congress Cataloging-in-Publication Number

2020942615

Typeset by Integra Software Services, Pondicherry
Print production managed by Jellyfish
Printed and bound by CPI Group (UK) Ltd, Croydon CR0 4YY

Dedicated to my late mum, my daughters, and all the women who will make the world work better.

And my husband too.

Contents

About the author

Rita Clifton started her career in advertising, becoming vice chairman and strategy director at Saatchi & Saatchi in its most successful period, and was London CEO and then Chairman at the global brand consultancy Interbrand over a 15-year stint. She has advised leading businesses around the world, as well as start-ups and growth-stage businesses of all shapes and sizes. In 2013, she co-founded the business and brand consultancy BrandCap, which she recently sold on to the management group.

She is a regular commentator across all media, including CNN, BBC, Sky and social channels, as well as a columnist. She was recently a mentor and judge on the CNBC award-winning series *Pop Up Start Up.*

She is a non-executive director on the boards of businesses including ASOS and Nationwide Building Society, and previously Bupa and Dixons Retail plc. Her non-profit work has included being a board trustee of WWF (Worldwide Fund for Nature) and a member of the UK government's Sustainable Development Commission.

Rita received a CBE for services to the advertising industry in 2014.

She is the author of best-selling books including *The Future of Brands* and two editions of *The Economist: Brands and Branding*. This time, it's more personal, and *Love Your Imposter* is a book she has been wanting and meaning to write for some time. It builds on her experience of leading, coaching and mentoring, and captures her own unique take and tips on how to get on and make your own difference in the world. She feels strongly that we need new kinds of (very human) leadership and many (many) more women running organizations of all kinds.

There's just a small matter of how…

Prologue
In my imposter dreams...

I've always been a bit of a dreamer. Not always in a good way.

Aside from the ballet dancer and saving-the-world stuff of daydreams, I've also managed to have the full range of anxiety dreams pretty much all my life. My own imposter has been alive and kicking both day and night.

Obviously, most of those dreams don't make sense, but I can guarantee that they will involve any or all elements of:

- being in a plane that can't take off high enough or brushes tall sliver-like buildings;
- being chased by someone/something of varying degrees of weirdness;
- having to retake exams when I haven't revised/make a presentation that I'm completely unprepared for.

And, of course, more often than not ending up stark naked. Usually in front of crowds of people. You don't need to delve into the book of Meaningful Anxiety Dreams for the symbolism.

I know I'm not alone. Apparently between 50 and 85 per cent of people claim to have (or rather, remember) these kinds of anxiety dreams and nightmares.[1] And women seem to experience these slightly more than men.

One of many theories is that they're apparently to do with something called 'threat simulation'. That people 'rehearse' frightening situations in their dreams, and this equips them to face those situations better in real life. (Mmm... fighting your way through writhing snakes on the floor, anyone?)

The same academic study also found that the students who had the most anxiety dreams the night before an exam scored the highest marks.[2]

This 50–85 per cent 'dream' figure is also broadly similar to those claiming to have imposter syndrome at work (c. 70 per cent of people, and around 90 per cent in creative industries).

And recently, there has been something of a torrent of actors, celebrities and business leaders talking about their insecurities and personal imposters.

Good for their honesty. And, judging by the success of so many of these people, it can often be used in a positive way.

Whether you personally have exactly the same feelings and experiences, a few things emerged from discussing some of these issues with others:

a That imposter syndrome is so common that it ceases to feel like a syndrome and starts to feel like a normal part of the human condition.

b People were very keen that I should be as honest as possible about the 'I'm a bit crap, me' feelings that lots of us have from time to time.

c Many of these worries and insecurities in dreams and in general are also normal... and can, in fact, be great sources of empathy with other human beings.

Which is funny, because a bit more honesty, empathy and basic humanity are just what business and the world needs at the moment. I hope that means you.

In fact, you can use some of this kind of personal stuff to help you (and, indeed, people and things around you) to shine and make it to the top. And as you, yourself. Not some corporate construct.

We're obviously all different, and this book is not intended as a self-help prescription. It's a collection of experiences, ideas and (yes, sorry…) tips that I've picked up along the way of life. I offer them as a *smorgasbord* – please feel free to do your own pick 'n' mix. They've evolved over time, and are a bit messy, in a way that life is. That felt normal too.

I have worked around the branding industry for most of my career, so have used several elements of brand thinking and building your personal brand as a way to help make things happen for you.

However, this book is not all about a highly self-conscious and laser-like focus on your personal brand throughout your career, whereby you plan your clear path up the mountain, kicking ass as you go. That's not life as we know it, and it's not particularly human.

So yes, *Love Your Imposter* is an open book, on all levels. There's a bit of theory, and a lot of practice. I've loved writing it, and I hope you find some things that might be useful.

Introduction

*Why this book, why now, and why
I'm writing it*

When I first thought about this book some years ago, its original working title was actually *Naked and Unprepared*. That started as a joke but reflected a truth. Throughout my personal and working life, I can honestly say I have never felt well-enough prepared for anything – whether an exam, school play, meeting, pitch, presentation or whatever. I'm always worried that I haven't done enough, haven't worked hard enough, haven't achieved enough and that, yes, someone's going to find me out. The imposter.

There are various definitions of Imposter Syndrome (both academic and more personal). A typical one from *Harvard Business Review* is 'a collection of feelings of inadequacy that persist despite evident success'.[1] To me, my imposter is that annoying feeling that tells me that this time, this time, is almost certainly going to be the time when everything goes pear-shaped in what I am about to do – and usually, in front of lots of people. The voice that says I'm probably not up to the job and should step aside for someone who really knows what they're doing. That's my experience, and you may well have your own invisible imposter friend or foe. In fact, it's both a relief and frustration that imposter syndrome is something shared by around 70 per cent of humanity.[2] It can certainly be exhausting. But these feelings can be useful in weird and interesting ways.

The book title eventually got changed to *Love Your Imposter* because my (very lovely) publisher was worried that people might get the wrong end of the (rude) stick from *Naked and Unprepared*. Both titles reflect the same sentiments: we can all feel exposed (and even dream about that quite literally), and we can all worry that we're not prepared or good enough... but that's a normal human thing. And the world needs decent humans in charge.

Despite so many women asking me to write an honest book about women and leadership that reflected real-life experiences, even during the process of writing I blew hot and cold about whether anyone would actually buy it/read it/like it/get anything from it. At a rather crucial 'downer' point in 2018, I attended an interesting lecture evening with the pioneering politician Dame Shirley Williams and the distinguished historian Niall Ferguson. The broad subject was about leadership, and I got talking to a rather brilliant, inspiring woman, who I later discovered was Vicky Gosling OBE and who was involved in founding and growing the Invictus Games. After a few minutes, she said, 'You're Rita Clifton, aren't you? I saw you speak at that leadership session a few years ago, and you absolutely changed my life.'

Yikes. That's quite a responsibility, I thought nervously… Anyway, she proceeded to tell me how, and how much she had appreciated my honesty.

It made me cry (in a good way). And then get on with finishing this book.

There is also the extra irony on the 'unprepared' front. Since I finally, finally got around to writing, there has been an explosion of great books by and about women in leadership, with demands for new ways of working and calls for radical change to the current system. I carried on in the spirit of more grist to an important mill, and in the hope that an extra-large helping of personal honesty might add something.

My other main motivation for finally getting around to writing the book was a Big Birthday. And whilst 50 might be the new 30, or 60 the new 40, these are times that you get to in your life when you mind slightly less about what people might think. You can be more honest about how things really are, rather than how we tend to present them as being.

And, of course, the other Big Thing that happened since I originally started thinking about this book is the #MeToo movement. It's been seriously gratifying to see how many women have been able to call out toxic behaviour, to be heard, and for real things to be done about it. In addition, in the UK, companies of all kinds have to report, account for and demonstrate what they are doing in terms of diversity, equality, pay gaps and generally better behaviour. It's good to be able to report some progress about making the business world more human and empathetic.

All I would say is that, despite all this good stuff, as I write this book we still have overt chauvinists in high office around the globe and women all over the world chucked in prison for saying and doing stuff that should be their right to say and do. The fight for inequality hasn't gone away. Indeed, in some cases, misogyny has skulked and festered underground.

In 2017, the World Economic Forum said that, at its current rate of progress, it would take 100 years to close the equality gap between men and women. And that women had just 68 per cent of the chances and outcomes that men have. The same research showed that women would have to wait 217 years before they earn as much as men and are equally represented in the workplace.[3] The number of female CEOs in the *Fortune* 500 companies actually went backwards by 25 per cent between 2017 and 2018 (even if it just about recovered in 2019).[4]

Women still need all the available avenues to ensure they get to run stuff – and right now, as well as in the future when we have truly changed systems.

There are obviously many ways of capturing the 'business castle'. Perhaps by a continuous siege or full-frontal on the ramparts (and with the support of all the #metoo equivalents for business and equality movements). Or perhaps by entering in disguise, doing the Trojan horse equivalent before you take the 'king' hostage and grab the proverbial crown. Or maybe even by sneaking up the drains by night. Otherwise, there's always the option of starting a new settlement elsewhere (if you can get the land and planning permission).

Enough analogies already. We can use all and any of these routes to get more women in charge.

It wasn't me...

Talking to others about imposter syndrome, whether male or female, I have been struck by people's different responses. Many will admit to similar feelings – even if they show up differently from the slightly freaky dreams I have. Some look blankly and start to shuffle away.

Studies show that two-thirds of women in the UK suffer from imposter syndrome at work.[5] It also affects almost 90 per cent of people in the creative industries. It isn't just a female thing, even though women are apparently 18 per cent more likely to feel it than men. Research suggests a number of reasons for this: that women's success is contraindicated by societal expectations; that women tend to be more self-critical in general; and even that women are prepared to be more open with their feelings and emotions.[6] (By contrast, because of social expectations, similar studies show men feel less able to be open about these issues and there is also apparently a hormonal 'testosterone effect', making men feel a greater sense of confidence.)

Whatever the causes, that's quite a lot of imposters knocking around.

It feels more like a syndrome of being human.

It's personal

Over the years I've been asked to give corporate speeches about brands, branding, marketing, communications and general business management. But I've also been asked to share my story at numerous conferences, business schools and sixth forms, to young executives as well as board peers. The organizers ask me to be as honest, open and personal as I can be.

I've been happy to do that in private sessions, but I've never shared my speech afterwards, because, well, it was personal.

Coming out as human

I'm now at a stage where I think we should come out as the flawed human beings that we all actually are. Like most people, I have made lots of mistakes (and still do). But there's a broader issue. Our media and public climate, especially in the UK, has elevated cynicism to a fine art, often characterizing and caricaturing people in big business as soulless, even Hollywood-type villains.

Sometimes, of course, people do ask for it. The business community has not helped its cause by too often behaving like an Alien Nation. Many senior executives still wear suits and ties, a working uniform that sets them apart. They can speak in stiff business jargon and look and sound as though they're from a different planet. And executive pay is truly out of this world.

It's up to all of us to change that conversation and bring it down to earth.

Trust me, I'm a business person

The declining trust in business and institutions has provoked a fair amount of soul-searching amongst business leaders.

In the 2019 Edelman Trust Barometer, only 56 per cent of the general public say they trusted business, a figure that declines to 53 per cent when answered solely by women.[7]

I've spoken at many business conferences and dinners on this trust deficit – one even had an archbishop as a guest speaker. We had a serious conversation about how Pope Francis had re-positioned the Catholic faith by humbling himself to his followers through symbolic actions like washing their feet. There was some agreement that businesses needed to do the equivalent. Businesses only succeed by the grace of the customer and the public and they need to serve them properly, and behave responsibly, in order to benefit from their ongoing support.

Despite the well-meaning sentiment of these gatherings, many conversations revolve around the senior leaders' view that business just needs to be 'better at communicating' what it does and what it brings to society; ie jobs, innovation to improve people's lives, and of course, wealth. Quite a lot of people might even agree in theory, but the problem is, they also believe that too much of the wealth remains with senior executives… whom they don't think deserve as much.

It's certainly not just about 'communications'.

The unacceptable face of inequality

There is a growing consensus that inequality is truly out of control and yes, something has had to give. That has shown up in populist events like the outcome of the Brexit referendum, the election of Donald Trump, the rise of angry nationalism and even the return of support for Marxism. But what do business leaders expect when wealth is increasingly sucked up to the top?

The inequality of income growth between the top and bottom earners of society is striking across the world. In all countries, income growth is systematically higher for upper income groups. In China, the lower earners' income growth between 1980 and 2016 was 417 per cent versus more than 3,750 per cent for the top 0.001 per cent. The gap between the lower 50 per cent and the top 0.001 per cent is even more marked in Russia (–26 per cent versus more than 25,269 per cent).[8]

The differential pay package ratio between a CEO and the average member of staff was over 300 in 2018 in US corporations, compared to 30 in the 1960s.[9] Meanwhile, most of the risk is pushed down to those who can least afford it, whilst the employment and financial advantages of senior executives are better protected. How would many senior executives feel about being a 'gig worker' with all the insecurity that brings to life?

This inequality is a very large elephant in a very public room.

And even if it has become more acceptable to talk about these issues in board remuneration committees over the past few years, there is still the danger of coming across as a hippy communist if you seek to address it.

Very few will vote for unilateral disarmament when it comes to reducing executive pay; as a board member you don't want to lose your best talent to competitors and do commercial self-harm at the altar of gesture, any more than turkeys (senior executives themselves) want to vote for a Christmas that reduces their remuneration.

At the World Economic Forum in 2016, the year when the Edelman survey hit peak distrust, 60 per cent of wealthy participants trusted organizations to do the right thing, versus 46 per cent of people on a lower income.[10]

People pick up their cues and clues about what's really going on from what people do rather than what they say. Reputation is reality with a lag effect. If you want people to think something different about you, you usually have to *do* something different.

Behaviour *is* communication.

All this is a problem for business because bad behaviour leads populist governments to need to be seen to control it through more overt business regulation – even if that's counter-productive for economies. It should be a source of shame and frustration for business that politicians know that they'll get more votes from giving (usually big) business a good kicking. It's bad news for business and bad news for its beneficial effects on society which get downplayed or underestimated.

The need to be human after all

All of this matters, because it adds up to a public perception of business as an inhuman place. Pantomime business programmes such as *The Apprentice* and *Dragons' Den* don't help. If people really behaved like that in business, you'd be in employment tribunals before you could say YOU'RE FIRED! Not to mention the loss of morale and goodwill; you can't buy people's enthusiasm, optimism and personal commitment if you scare and bully them senseless.

We need business to be more human. To be something positive that all human beings either work in or get paid by (and so should encourage and support). And we really, really need businesses to be sustainably successful if we're to generate the kind of money we need to pay for schools, hospitals and civil society.

Businesses need to behave as though the rest of the world matters… because it does.

It's all very well to say that a business is only responsible to shareholders, but this becomes a proxy for making as much short-term profit as possible. The longer-term responsibilities of business – to generate sustainable wealth that employs people reliably and looks after customers – are as fundamentally important. It's also worth remembering that shareholders themselves aren't just faceless institutions. They're staff, pensioners, ordinary people with savings and a stake in society. And if we don't have clean air to breathe, if there are no resources left and the majority lead miserable lives, who cares what the quarterly results say?

HUMANS VERSUS ALIENS

Successful people who present as more human than the corporate suit brigade tend to have a more sympathetic hearing:

- Think Richard Branson, at least in the early days (Failed school! Dyslexic! Wore rubbish cardigans!)

- Think Usain Bolt (Stuffed himself with chicken nuggets! Likes to party!)

- People even got to like *Dragons' Den* entrepreneur Deborah Meaden when she showed her vulnerable, funny,

---

> self-deprecating side (versus her grumpy frowny caricature) on *Strictly Come Dancing*. Similarly with Ed Balls, the former UK politician. Gangnam Style will never be the same.
>
> - Other very human examples include Indra Nooyi (inspiring CEO and general human), Oprah (enough said) and Bill Gates. Anyone who saw him trying to dance on stage at the launch of Windows in 1995 would have a heart of stone if you didn't want to hug him and make it stop.[11] It does help, of course, that he has donated $45.5 billion to health and social causes through his foundation.

Changing business for good

The world needs changing; business runs the world; so we need to change business.

To me, that means being more human.

That means business people acting more like human beings who have families, partners, pets, consciences, pulses. Even a sense of humour.

It means stopping pretending they know everything (and only talking privately about how they would really like to do more good if only they could convince their shareholders).

It is a bit better now than when I started in business, but looking at some of the PR gaffes, and the disdain with which some business leaders are perceived to have treated staff and customers, there's still a long way to go. You will have your own 'favourite' examples, but these cases come to mind:

- United Airlines (customer forcibly dragged off a plane, CEO initially blames customer, then resorts to defensive jargon);

- Uber (various allegations, including sexual discrimination and harassment lawsuits, leading to the founder/CEO stepping down);
- Persimmon CEO in the UK (takes £85 million bonus, even though it was inflated by a taxpayer-funded scheme. Walks off TV interview when asked about it).

All of these examples were obviously highlighted and magnified by social media; there's an added imperative on doing the right thing now that we operate in a digital world. In the pre-digital days, if a business was full of people behaving badly, there was a chance you could get away with it if you had a decent PR department and lots of money to spend on good marketing. Now, you get found out with a scale and speed that takes your breath away. Social media and anonymous employee review sites like Glassdoor ensure whatever happens inside gets outside in a flash. Today, there's no substitute for being a great business, where people care about their work, who like and believe in what they do, and are prepared to tell others. This is cheap and effective marketing too. Big, bad, lazy businesses have a lot to sweat about.

Be your best self

So yes, we need to be more human in the best ways. Although, having said that, I find the advice to just 'be yourself' to succeed at work a bit unnerving. No one really needs to know that you like hanging around in your dressing gown eating snacks and watching daytime television when you're 'working from home'.

Despite its over-use, I prefer the term being your 'best self' – ie a normal human being, with emotions, trying to do the right thing, even if you're not always certain whether you've got the right answer. Sharing something honest about yourself and/or what you've done wrong can also help people understand and at least try to do the right thing in their own situation. In the end, do what's best to make the most of your good self and those around you.

It's always about people

If the key to successful and sustainably valuable businesses is to build good, long-term and reliable customer relationships, then you need to start using language and behaviour from respectful human relationships rather than sharp and exploitative practice.

When asked about the original success of her business at a speech she gave at one of my previous companies, the late, great Anita Roddick, founder of The Body Shop said, 'We advertised for employees, but people turned up instead.' She knew that to build a sustainable business you had to care for the people who worked for you, and recognize them as sentient beings with messy feelings, emotions and needs. Unilever, Patagonia and some of the more enlightened global brands are doing the same.

Similarly, I'm allergic to the generic term 'The Consumer'. I don't recognize this single entity. But what I do know is that different kinds of people consume different kinds of brands. None of these terms like 'The Staff', 'The Consumer', 'The Public' create a sense of human connection. If you use these terms you're reducing people to 'third-party' specimens to be observed and exploited, and that's not what's needed.

I'm struck by how many people are fabulously human, funny, caring and self-deprecating in private, but as soon as they put a business suit on, or have the cameras rolling, up go the shoulders, on goes the 'professional' face and language and we are left with the corporate husk again.

Chemistry lessons about leadership

To achieve the transformation we want in business, we need a change of chemistry at the top – literally and emotionally. This is my not very subtle code for having many, many more women running our major organizations and institutions around the world. Here I'll also include a load of start-ups and organizations of all shapes and sizes.

This is not to say that men can't 'do human', or that women have the monopoly on EQ (emotional intelligence). But rather, things work better when they're balanced. I won't repeat all the excellent learning from books like Sheryl Sandberg's *Lean In*, Helena Morrissey's *Good Time to be a Girl*, or the wonderful Mary Portas' *Work Like a Woman*. Or indeed all the studies that demonstrate that having more women on boards and at senior management levels leads to greater sustainable performance and less risk.[12]

But a quick example.

Organizations in the top 25 per cent for gender diversity among executive leadership teams were more likely to outperform on profitability (21 per cent) and value creation

(27 per cent), according to McKinsey & Company's study of 1,000 companies in 12 countries.[13]

One of my favourite pieces of research on the positive effect of more balanced workforces was into NASA astronauts, who were asked about the impact of female astronauts on the space programme. Some 75 per cent of them were really positive, and said that it led to 'calmer missions', 'better language' and 'better personal hygiene'.[14] Well, I think we'll have that for starters. The boardroom can sometimes be a pretty dirty place too.

It was fascinating to attend a lunch with Sheryl Sandberg, COO of Facebook. I know she's had some bad rap since the publication of *Lean In* because of allegations about Facebook's corporate practices, but she has also suffered from tragic personal trauma. She was a great and very human speaker. What stuck in my mind is that she recited all the statistics about how totally dominated the leadership of the working and political worlds are by men... and then said with fabulous understatement, 'And it doesn't seem to be going that well...'.

Business in the new real world

I want business and businesses of all kinds, shapes and sizes, to succeed. Because we all need them to pay for and support – *and be part of* – a humane and civilized society. A lot of us can spend most of our waking moments 'at work' and increasingly, being 'digitally on' means that a part of us is always there, so it's a true waste if we don't all deliberately set out to make sure work works for us, our colleagues and our lives in the round.

I'm not sure we should talk about 'business *and* society' as two separate concepts. It's business *in* society, playing its role of providing interesting and productive work that helps people and helps society. And yes, provides *proportionate* wealth for those prepared to take risks and responsibility for starting and leading successful businesses.

Why a pick 'n' mix approach to advice?

On the relative 'shit to shine' front, my career has turned out OK, in a way that has surprised me and certainly surprised my director of studies at university. I've worked with, or for, some high-profile companies, including Saatchi & Saatchi in its most successful period. I've run and chaired a global brand consultancy (and started a new one), and been lucky enough to sit on the boards of some interesting businesses as well as amazing charities (like WWF).

Bizarrely, I've facilitated a leadership discussion between a former Archbishop of Canterbury, the head of the Muslim Council of Great Britain and the head of the Armed Forces. I've made speeches from Shanghai to Sydney via Sweden, South Africa, Singapore and Santiago. I told the broadcaster and natural historian Sir David Attenborough in front of 200 people that I have had a crush on him since I was seven and I have made a vote of thanks to Melinda Gates: this was scary stuff, but she was fabulous and very down to earth. Similarly, I thought I was going to expire from nerves for a speech to Hillary Clinton but she was brilliant and I survived.

One of my proudest moments was when I received the Commander of the Most Excellent Order of the British Empire honour, otherwise known as a CBE, from HM Queen Elizabeth II in 2015, and my Mum was sitting only 10 steps away from the Queen. Sadly, my Mum has died since then, but she could never stop talking about it afterwards. This was an extraordinary experience for her, being one of 12 children who spent her working life as a shop assistant and cleaning lady. She was also widowed at an early age too – my Dad died when he was only 51. She was just 45 and I was 12.

As far as my own less extreme experience is concerned, I've done the stuff I've done whilst having more than a small dose of human frailty and a large dose of self-doubt. As I said at the beginning of the book, my imposter has been a constant companion, and I've slightly grudgingly got to know and even appreciate its presence.

I don't think I've got a magic formula for success, and I'm not setting out to make grand claims. I've written this book because I wanted to share what I've learned, and would like to dedicate this book to helping other people to lead and start businesses with flaws and all – and see those as being advantages.

I will be using bits of my life as a backdrop, not because I think it is particularly interesting or unusual – everyone's is, in some way – but because it provides some narrative and excuse to share real experiences.

Clearly, everyone is different. Everything I say has the benefit of looking through the rear-view mirror. I have never been very good at taking my own advice and the book is a collection of my thoughts and observations. Please feel free to pick your own takeaways, and to ignore anything that doesn't suit you, even inwardly heckle if you so choose (but ideally after reading the chapter on Nice Guys…).

First, I'm going to be talking about what we can learn, even from the early years of being pretty **Clueless**, followed by some examples of how to get it more together (**Groundwork**), and then exploring why and how we're affected by appearances and certain events (**Hairy Moments and Happier Outcomes**). I'm then going to tackle how to ensure you know the harder-edged numerical stuff about getting more senior, and really knowing what's going on (**Magic Numbers and Difficult Statistics**, as well as **Money Talks**), and some personal experiences on how (and how not) to be your best self at work at any stage (**Why You Don't Have to Fake It to Make It**). Next, a few hints and tips on communicating and being as influential as you can be (**Voices Off**), and then some suggestions about how to get more skills and opportunities… as well as dealing with potentially angsty issues like having a family (**Extending Skills and Expanding Your Life**). The last three chapters are devoted to how to keep progressing in a way that suits you (**Women Rule OK**), with some final advice and musings on how being an asshole (or living with one) is a bad idea in **Nice Guys Don't Finish Last**. The last chapter is about what business could do and be like in the future if we're all to get more out of it for common good – and how you can use your personal brand to help make good things happen (**You and The Future Of Business**). The **Epilogue** is just the latest in real life… .

CHAPTER ONE

Clueless

On my own imposter backstory

I f I'm to share real-life thoughts and experiences in a way that's authentic and gives some context for the rest of the book, that also means sharing a bit about my earlier life. It is not particularly out of the ordinary, but I hope that, if nothing else, it reinforces the old English colloquial phrase, 'there's nowt so queer as folk', meaning that there's nothing as strange as the variety of people.

Clearly, many people have terrible, heart-breaking backgrounds and life experiences, and for no fault of their own, are crushed by them. They deserve all the support people can give to overcome them. I take my hat off to those who come through and make a positive difference to others.

Then there are those who have slightly odd back stories (most of us, seemingly), and who might value a few thoughts to use that slight oddness to help achieve as much as they can.

A bit of my backstory...

I was born the last child of a man who'd injured his back whilst delivering a huge pallet of bread. My Mum was seven months pregnant, with two small children already, and an ambulance turned up with my Dad groaning on a stretcher and dumped him at home. They were living in a caravan at the time because they'd been kicked out of their flat after my Dad's latest business attempt – a dry-cleaning company – folded.

When he got worse, they called the ambulance again and discovered that his back was broken. He was basically an invalid all the time I knew him.

Giving it all away

My father was, however, pretty smart. He came from a mining village just outside Newcastle-upon-Tyne in the north-east of England and most of his male relatives worked down the coal mines while his mother eventually ran the local post office. Dad was the product of an affair in the Great War of 1914–18. His mum became pregnant by an Army ambulance driver posted nearby; they quickly married and Arthur Senior (his dad) went off to war, where he died before even meeting his son. Just one of many similar sad tales, I know.

My father then did really well at school and he especially enjoyed telling me later that he often got 99 per cent and 100 per cent for exams, particularly when I only got 97 per cent. He even allegedly sat for a scholarship for the London School of Economics, but sadly for him was never able to take up a place because he, in turn, became a father when he was 18. That relationship didn't last long and he then married an actress and had two more children. That also broke down in the face of my Dad's seeming inability to be a reliable husband. (Did I mention he was a compulsive gambler?) In the following years, he moved to Surrey, having dispensed with his regional Geordie accent after merciless teasing in the Royal Air Force. Soon after the Second World War he eventually found himself at a dance where he broke into a waltz with my mother. He offered her nylon stockings and she was smitten.

Mum was one of 12 children, 10 girls and two boys (later in life, it was like being amongst a litter of cats with all my aunties). She had to leave school aged 14 to earn money and was, of course, seriously impressed by my charming and clever Dad-to-be. Her parents were minor musical theatre entertainers; her father was actually an aircraft engineer by trade by day, but his first love was the stage. Grandma ran away from boarding school around the turn of the last century and became an artist's model, featuring in *Tatler* and *Harper's Bazaar* magazine. Again, *nowt so queer as folk*.

Dad eventually confessed he had been married twice before, but he and Mum made it marriage number three, and after two more children together, I was his third (or sixth, depending on how you look at it) and definitely last child.

I won't go into Dad's various jobs, businesses and schemes, but suffice to say, he was not an easy employee or businessman because work got in the way of his gambling. Fortunately, my previously flighty and flirty Mum turned out to be a grafter, and it was she who managed to sew, run the dry-cleaning shop, and clean houses to keep the show on the road.

It's funny how you can take things for granted, but I am sure that in some way the fact that my poor Mum was working the clock round both in and out of the home made me feel that it was normal to do so. I also later discovered that with all the strain of my ill father, three young children, constant money troubles and undiagnosed anaemia, she had a nervous breakdown when I was very young. She was away for months in a mental health hospital whilst we stayed with my grandmother. I don't remember anything specific, but do have the vague memory of an undefined, aching longing as a toddler. Anyway, I'm still breathing. My daughters now laugh at me whenever I smother them with love.

You'll have your own experiences to bring to bear. The important thing is to recognize them, their impact and try to use them in a positive way.

We're all products of our time to some extent, but whether post-war, liberation, big shoulders, or #MeToo era, the eternal truth is that every generation of women does what they can and what they need to do.

Here I am

You may well recognize which characteristics you've got from which parent, and I seem to have inherited a blend from mine. I got a decent academic brain from Dad, a responsible streak from Mum (as well as a love of dancing), and a lifelong aversion to risk and gambling. Which is even more fortunate, because when Dad surreptitiously took me to the horse races when he was supposed to be childminding, I was blissfully oblivious to the fact that he NEEDED to be there, whereas I thought we were just looking at the lovely horses. I did, though, manage to study racehorse form like an academic subject; to be honest, there wasn't much else to read in our house except *Timeform* horse racing books. However, to my everlasting gratitude, there was a set of 10 green encyclopaedias. I don't know what possessed my father to buy these, except that he did enjoy me being clever and I found out lots of stuff about astronomy, the dinosaurs and myths.

The only other book I remember in my parents' house was *How to Be a Barrister*. This appeared random, except when I discovered that Dad had bought it to sue his bread delivery employers for damages to his back. I don't know the full ins and outs, aside from the fact that he managed to get enough compensation for a leasehold on a small shop in a village called Bourne End, near Marlow, in Buckinghamshire. It was a vinyl record and toy shop and, hey, I was the daughter of a shopkeeper!

I used to hang around in the shop every Saturday and school holidays, although I didn't realize that this was, in fact, my parents' necessary version of babysitting. I was quite good at maths and used to add up the weekly takings on the till roll. However, what appeared on the till roll bore little resemblance to what we actually earned because a rather large (fatherly) hand used to delve into the till every week to spend on the horses. Bills often went unpaid, but because we often 'borrowed' toys from the shop and had food, my siblings and I were under the impression that life was pretty OK.

Real life becomes a nightmare

I would possibly have remained in blissful ignorance. I passed the 11-plus exam to go to the local grammar school, and I had dancing lessons and horse riding so that Dad could pretend we were more affluent.

But then, he got sick, then sicker, then went into hospital for a check-up. Suddenly, Mum was called to the hospital in the middle of the night. I had a strange dream and woke suddenly with a heart wrench.

He was dead. He was only 51, my sister and brother were 19 and 14 respectively and I was 12. Mum was 45 and totally pole-axed.

It was truly awful. Every year I have been alive since my younger daughter was 12 (she's now in her 20s) has felt like a bonus. If this sounds a bit morbid, I remember talking to a business colleague many years later at a rather deep and meaningful offsite session, and she confessed that she had lost her father in a plane crash when she was a toddler.

She had always come across as a bit pessimistic and cynical in her outlook and now I knew why – she readily admitted that it was difficult to throw herself with overt enthusiasm into anything. When you've lost someone so precious so young, and seen its impact on others, you can keep yourself and your emotions buttoned up for ever more. But this conversation led to a whole new way of us working together, when she could openly acknowledge that, maybe it was just her, but these were the things that she felt were wrong with our business. Her caution was *valuable* in the right context, and a real advantage to me and the company.

I am sure you know lots of people with similar revelations. Sharing a little bit of a personal story can be quite liberating if it's relevant and doesn't take up too much of someone's day.

There were also a few other things that my father's early death made me realize – even years later.

PRINCESSES AND DUCKLINGS

A women's executive network organization in the UK once conducted an interesting qualitative study into the backgrounds and key characteristics of a wide range of successful women in business. It was almost 25 years ago, but one part really stuck in my mind. Amongst many other more nuanced findings, they also found that their interviewees roughly identified into two camps. The study termed these 'Daddy's Princesses' and 'Ugly Ducklings'.

Daddy's Princesses – these were described as women who had felt loved, cherished and supported (particularly by their fathers) from an early age, and tended to grow up believing that they were indeed 'worth it', scoring life and academic goals with relative ease and who grew up almost wondering what the problem was.

Ugly Ducklings – these were the other interviewees who, for whatever reason, did not feel as loved or valued by one or both of their parents, but responded to the negativity by trying to prove their worth and success; they may have found it more difficult to achieve personal happiness but the rise to the top of organizations showed their determined mettle.

The terms feel rather clumsy for today, but it's interesting how the fundamental importance of the relationship between parent and daughters – both good and bad – maps on to other academic studies about successful women.[1]

Know thyself

In real life, many people can be driven by a mix of these positive and negative effects and emotions, and the difference is how each individual responds. I have known people who had such idealized expectations of a life partner that they were totally shocked when they found they had shacked up with a serial cheater. Equally, so-called 'ugly ducklings' become determined that they would do the opposite of how they were brought up.

I do believe that people can make use of life experiences if they have proper support. I also know it's tempting to look at people with a 'bootstraps up' mindset, and judge others, particularly if you had a bit of a hard time yourself. However, it's worth remembering that not everyone can 'pull themselves together' without help and belief. It should be part of all our agendas to help others – and remember our own impact if and when we have children ourselves.

From a personal point of view, I guess I had a blend of both 'princess' and 'duckling' in my upbringing. I did feel adored by my father, but that was rudely cut off by his death before my adolescence. And I later discovered that my rosy picture of him didn't reflect the flawed man. His death also exposed me to some experiences in my teens that challenged my confidence and security. But the effort to impress a dead parent and create stability and security perversely turned out to be a useful motivator for me. There's lots of research about how losing a parent in early life is correlated with later business and career drive.

In his book *David and Goliath*, Malcolm Gladwell dubs this group 'Eminent Orphans' and says that the death of a mother or father is a spur. Because you are on your own, the book suggests you are forced to persist, to invent, to chart your own way.[2] In addition to business leaders and entrepreneurs who are disproportionately represented in 'orphans', Gladwell also discovered that 67 per cent of British prime ministers from the start of the 19th century to the beginning of the Second World War lost a parent before the age of 16, and 12 US presidents all lost their fathers when they were young. If you're some kind of orphan, you're in good if tragic company.

A small compensation, though, as I am sure most of us would have forgone that kind of 'success' to have the parent back.

Another impact of my father leaving us very much in debt was the reality of having absolutely no money unless we earned it. My poor mother tried to carry on the family shop for a year or so but couldn't manage. She took a part-time job in a bakery, and I worked every weekend and school holiday in the old shop, now bought by someone else. I have to confess that it did have some advantages in that I met a lot of potential boyfriends in the record department... .

When the shop work wasn't available any more, you name it, I worked in it: factories, offices, laboratories, pubs, clubs. I became an expert on all the local temporary employment agencies, and enjoyed the variety of people I met, and gained a greater understanding of so many different lives.

Years later, with my own children, even though as a parent you always want to protect them from any discomfort or unpleasantness, we did find that working in a series of unglamorous weekend and holiday jobs was great life experience for them. If ever they needed it, it taught them NEVER to take anyone or anything for granted – and to try and grit teeth and smile through when they need to.

Again, I've put my back story in for context, but it drives a few broader observations for me:

- Everyone's family is unique in some way. We've all got skeletons in the closet, and whether you choose to parade them or not, you can actively seek to manage whether they drive you positively or negatively.
- It's better not to make rash assumptions about people, because you can't know their personal stories.
- Try and help everyone you can to make use of their background and experiences in a positive way.

The above may obviously need some professional intervention, and I talk more about this in Chapter 6.

The ups and downs of schooldays

After a strange period at school, where I went from top of the class to a spotty and hunched teenager with a hitched-up skirt, trying to sneak on make-up, I was eventually helped by a fierce, clever teacher who reckoned I could get into Cambridge University. It hadn't even occurred to me I would go to university.

There was a farcical moment where this particular teacher was inspecting my university application form, and particularly noting the passport photo I had attached.

She uttered these rather memorable words, 'For goodness' sake, Rita, you're supposed to look as though you know something about Classics, not like a Sex Queen'. This was 1975 after all, and I had the regulation panda eye make-up and gothic hair falling below my waist.

Nevertheless, I secured a place at Newnham College, Cambridge University to read Classics. This was (and still is) a specifically women-only college, but at that time in the wider university there were about six men to one woman. It's difficult even now to stay calm about some of the brilliant women from my school who should have had the chance to go, but there were not enough places for them.

I am sure my bright schoolfriends have all thrived, but the injustice at that time was hard to take. Even if the balance of students has shifted, business leaders are still in the old Cambridge proportions as far as gender is concerned.

Fortunately, having got angry, women have also got more than even in the education equality stakes in most parts of the Western world. In September 2017, an 18-year-old British woman was 36 per cent more likely to start a degree course than her male peers.[3] However, there's still quite a lot more to do in many other parts of the world.

Discovering an 'other' world

We obviously had no family car, so arriving at Cambridge for the first time, I was given a lift by my sister and her new husband. They had scraped the money together to buy a rusty old Morris Traveller. As I'm sure you can imagine it was nicely set off by the line of rather more expensive cars all dispensing female freshers.

I felt out of place in those early days as I met people with regal-sounding first names, double-barrelled last names and then the range of privately educated school boys. So many of them belonged to clubs that I'd never heard of, that I would never be invited to, and where people clearly knew each other. They were from an 'other' social world that didn't need anyone who came from a scruffy semi, had never skied, held her knife incorrectly and definitely had the Wrong Shoes. Having said all that, I met the most extraordinary people and several of these women became lifelong friends. I met the wonderful and forthright Mary Beard, who is now a high-profile broadcaster and feminist academic, and some other of the best brains and wits in the world.

If you don't mind, I will pass a veil over my academic achievements. As my Director of Studies said to me afterwards, 'Well, at least it wasn't a third', which in the British university system, is the lowest degree classification. In a written note she also said that I could have done so much better, that I had sometimes maddened and frustrated her, but actually, that she had never regretted taking me. I wept.

Strangely, that was not the last time she made me weep, and not in a bad way. She managed to drop me a few notes over the next 30 years making a few observations on my 'achievements' – inverted commas because inevitably, achieving anything in business was not necessarily what she or very many of the academic staff at Cambridge thought was proper. The last note from her was when I was awarded the CBE in 2014. True to tradition, she congratulated me, but then managed to reduce me to my rightful 19-year-old size by saying that she had watched my career with 'some surprise'.

But never underestimate the power of a letter. Even – if not more so – in a digital age.

Frankly, she wasn't the only one who was surprised. My career came as a complete surprise to me as well.

I attended her 80th birthday party, and when introducing me to someone else, she said, '… and this is Rita, who's become a *Captain of Industry*'. The way she spoke was as if she would only have been slightly more surprised if I had become an axe murderer. I should also say that I wanted to laugh out really loudly – not just because of the ludicrous comment, but also because the very thought that anyone would refer to me as a Captain of Industry made me want to howl.

It's a similar story to when the Right Honourable Virginia Bottomley, a British ex-government minister and with whom I was on the Cambridge Business School advisory board years later, asked me casually over a cup of tea, 'So, Rita, what do you think has made you so successful?'

It's no false modesty to say that I have NEVER thought of myself as very successful. When I have looked at myself in comparison with people whom I considered *properly* successful business people, I never feel that I have worked hard enough, done enough or achieved enough to deserve the 'success' word.

After a discussion, she and I agreed that, actually, it was quite helpful to never feel as though you had succeeded, because that provided a constant energy and drive to do more. So yes, this may be true, but honestly, it can be tiring.

Without wishing to be too clichéd, university was a truly transforming experience, and lifted my horizons. I'm not sure what from and to, because to be frank, I hadn't a clue what my horizons were or where I was going. Although one thing I was clear about was that I needed to earn some money. Preferably a reasonable amount, and as quickly as possible. I didn't know of the late, great entrepreneur Felix Dennis at the time (millionaire poet, publisher and author of *How to Get Rich*), but his obsession with taking risks and 'fuck the lot of them' would have been an alien concept to me.

Getting the first job: any job...

The Cambridge Careers Advisory Service at that time was a hilariously amateur affair, because, well, sophisticated people had the contacts to go into the City. (I didn't even know what that was beyond a caricature... which was probably pretty accurate, and it definitely didn't involve women of my dubious background.) Or they were going into the Civil Service, the BBC, drama school, or possibly finding the cure for cancer.

My ambitions were pretty vulgar and vague in comparison and I furtively filled in forms that didn't really belong in polite Cambridge society at the time: words like 'marketing' were kept to a whisper, and the distinctions between advertising, copywriting, media and sales were totally blurry. And so they remained, even while I was attending the graduate 'milk round' of company visits and interviews, where the best of UK commerce toured to the so-called best universities flogging graduate jobs.

Those were the days when there was an orderly selection of graduate schemes and jobs and the main way you prepared for interviews was trying not to have a hangover. It's so much more difficult these days and careers so much more fragmented and fragile, with the only alleviating factor that at least you can use the internet to prepare as opposed to fusty old library files.

During my various interviews, I did learn a few things, and was grateful to one particular person who interviewed me for a graduate role at Mars, part of the US conglomerate, Mars Inc, the chocolate and confectionery company.

He asked me why I wanted the graduate sales job (to be honest, I didn't really – I just wanted the company car and the very competitive salary on offer). I rambled a bit about liking selling, rambled a bit more about Mars being a well-known company, rambled more about other stuff. It was another (unnecessarily long) answer to some perfectly simple and sharp questions.

His eyes glazed over again, before he said, not unkindly, 'Rita – honestly, you talk too much'. I don't think he was trying to muzzle me for being a feisty woman. I just managed to bore him.

It hurt, though, and I was cross with myself.

But I used the advice at my next interview, where a couple of nice interviewers from Yellow Pages (who used to make those huge doorstep telephone directories) were asking me about my motivations for selling advertising in their huge doorstep telephone directories.

'Well,' I said, 'I think I've got a knack for selling, and I'm interested in advertising.'

And then I shut up.

They were taken so much by surprise with my sharp answer that they lost their place in their notes, looked at each other, laughed and then one said, 'Well, that's the best answer we've had so far.' I wasn't so staccato in my other answers, but I stood out and they offered me the job. I didn't take it, but there we are.

Good for the ego at a scary point in life.

The reason I chose media/marketing in the end was that:

a I didn't want to do any more exams (so farewell accountancy, despite the huge numbers they recruited);

b I wasn't academically shiny enough to do management consultancy (off with McKinsey, Bain, BCG);

c my very small-time stage experience in ballet and choreography, combined with customer service in pubs and shops could, weirdly, be presented in a useful way;

d what I had managed to read about this industry made it sound interesting to someone as nosy about people as me;

e and most of all, I got some actual job offers.

I realized that some of my work experiences with many different types of people were really quite useful. The combination of Cambridge, factory floors, a borrowed faux-fur coat and wearing too much make-up to interviews actually seemed intriguing to a few potential employers. I managed to end up working for the leading advertising agency in the UK at the time (sadly now defunct).

A veteran of interview trial and error by now, when one of the most senior interviewers asked me if I had any questions, I paused, looked steadily at him and said, 'So, am I someone that you would like to see working here?'. I didn't quite know what I meant, but I had cottoned on to the idea of saying something clear that made you stand out. He was momentarily flustered at the directness, but recovered enough to confess that, yes, I could well be the kind of person they wanted to hire this year.

In previous years, perhaps not so much. But he claimed that they were now seeking greater diversity.

I swallowed. That would be me.

I might have stupidly thought that copywriting was like signwriting (ie the signage above shops), and I may have had to borrow suitable clothes for the interview, but I was in. As a client manager. And earning £4,001 per annum (that's about £19,500 today).

Getting down to it

When I arrived, I quickly realized what the job was really about and fell down to earth with a bump. Despite fondly imagining that advertising was a glamorous business, my first accounts were marketing Harpic and Steradent. Toilet and denture cleaners weren't quite what I had in mind, but I learned another important lesson. You can honestly get interested in just about anything. Who knew that the consumer psychology involved in having a deeply clean bathroom to show visitors, and the 'one foot in the grave' emotions about getting your first denture could be so riveting?

The key lesson here is that, wherever you start, you learn a lot of things that will benefit you in your working life. Like, for instance:

- how to work with other people (who may or may not be difficult to work with);
- how to get up in the morning – every day;
- being reliable;
- not sulking even if people don't agree with you;
- what interests you and what drains you;
- a whole variety of roles are available in a whole variety of companies;
- don't agonize too long about the perfect job – it can all be very arbitrary, at least to begin with;
- just start something and somewhere – you can always swap later.

It can be a long and winding road.

It always throws me when I'm asked to speak on topics like 'Journey to CEO', as though I knew from the age of seven that I was going to run things. Like lots of people, my career has been a series of highways, byways and a couple of cul-de-sacs. I was genuinely clueless to begin with, but soon began to feel that I should get more clued up to avoid getting fired.

You may well feel that you have a clear plan, wherever you are in your life and career. All I would say is that, if you don't, don't stress too much. Even with an ill-defined drive to achieve something, things tend to happen.

NOTES TO SELF

- We're all weird in some way – try to view whatever background and life experiences you've had as positive drive and material (get help from books, mentors, friends or professionals if you can't do it yourself).

- If you don't like others judging you before they've understood you, don't do it to others. Helping people is a better use of energy.

- You can start your working life just about anywhere, and get interested in the most unexpected stuff. Be nosey about everything and everyone (including yourself).

CHAPTER TWO

Groundwork

On early lessons in working life, including a bit of personal branding

I f Cambridge was a transforming experience, working at Saatchi & Saatchi, the advertising agency, in the 1980s was a mind-blower.

My first job had been at a traditional, if very successful ad agency. It had an executive dining room where you had a couple of pre-prandial drinks, followed by a long lunch, supported by several glasses of wine, followed by the full port and cigars scenario. And yes, this was at midday.

I was a junior executive at the time, but when clients came to visit the agency, I was allowed to join them for lunch. In retrospect, I suspect that as a young woman in advertising, this was mainly for decoration purposes.

This may have been insulting, but at that stage I thought it was normal. After these lunches, I have no idea how I stayed awake during the afternoon.

In fact, I frequently didn't. My particular nadir was having a sleep in the ladies' bathrooms when I couldn't handle the drinking pace. Whilst at the same time, I was thinking 'Wow, all this food and drink is FREE! Must take full advantage.'

Oh, how things have changed.

In most businesses at that time, as a young woman real diversity was a galaxy far, far away. If nothing else, the recent #MeToo campaign should give us extra energy to make sure no other young women (or men for that matter) have to put up with what they have had to put up with while they're trying to get on in their working lives.

The main things I learned in that first proper 'executive' job were: it was a good idea to look after clients and people across all departments if you wanted to get on; and whether we like it or not, it does matter how you present yourself.

I'll be talking more about this 'presenting yourself' in later chapters, but I obviously mean a lot more than the 'stick-on' and superficial parts of appearance. I'm also talking about how you use your voice to get heard, how you hold yourself to get listened to, how you 'wear' your skills and knowledge to build confidence and empathy.

Wearing the wrong trousers (OK, skirt)...

By today's standards I got married relatively young. My honeymoon at 22 had been a rare European holiday and

I returned heavily tanned. I was keen to show this off and dressed down accordingly. The HR director was nicely insulting about what I was wearing. When I crossed his path in the corridor he looked me up and down and said, not unpleasantly, 'Where's the beach?' When I smiled cheerily, he then followed up with a fixed smile, 'Probably good to think about whether that's suitable for meetings if you want to come across as an executive.'

Part of me was thinking, 'How dare you. I want to be judged by who I am, what I think, what I can do, who I really am.' But honestly, it was to be some time before I had the faintest grip of any of these questions either.

It was an uncomfortable moment, and not something that should happen now. But I did smarten myself up by saving up for two suits. They actually made me feel a bit more professional, and act accordingly. I'll be talking more about this annoying phenomenon later.

For all my worries, I seemed to do well enough to attract the attention of a recruitment agency. This recruiter happened to be looking for an account manager at a rather fast-growing agency called Saatchi & Saatchi.

Waking up to real executive life

I found myself being grilled by some fearsomely bright, high-energy people about confectionery, skincare and why I'd like to work for the next number one ad agency in the world.

Even the reception area gave off a completely different vibe from the rather sleepy, nice atmosphere of my previous company. People came in and out and walked so fast across reception that everything looked speeded up. This was the first time the 'brand' thing really came home to me, if only I had realized it at the time. It's important to note that you pick up your cues and clues about any brand, whether ad agency, retailer, bank or plumber, from everything you see and experience about them.

The cut and thrust atmosphere of Saatchi's brand was a culture shock in every way after my cuddly warm bath of a first job. I had to worry about money and managing it, and yes, even making it for the company!

Of course, Saatchi's was a publicly quoted business on the London Stock Exchange and needed a handle on their finances all the time. I just hated the pressure and administrative burden – and I was also supposed to be managing a couple of people too.

My anxiety and awkwardness on the job was alleviated by sitting opposite a seemingly confident, slightly brooding Heathcliff-type guy. He was working on the chocolate part of the Rowntree Mackintosh advertising account (that's now Nestlé, and his brands were Quality Street and Rolo). I worked on the 'sugar' brands like Fruit Pastilles and Fruit Gums. It was all rather sweet. After a few months, I realized that I should actually be with him rather than the other very nice man I had married so young.

This all became a bit traumatic, on top of the stresses of a stressful job, so I left Saatchi's and ran away to a Greek Island for a few months of working holiday so I could 'find myself'. Perhaps even write that novel many of us think we have inside us.

As it turned out, I didn't write any such novels, but I did find that gazing out into a blue sea and looking after student tourists brought me to my senses. I can actually recommend a period of this kind of reflection at some point, whether a sabbatical, grown-up gap year, working holiday, retreat, whatever. It certainly puts things in perspective.

Take two

I did return to the UK and moved to the ad agency J Walter Thompson, which was then known as the 'university of advertising'. This was an intellectual, if not emotional eye-opener. It was the most sophisticated and upmarket of all the upmarket agencies at the time, and I found myself buying fake pearls and smart blazers to fit in. If I could easily have changed my name from Rita to something more patrician, I would have seriously considered it.

I'll be looking at the whole 'faking it' concept later in Chapter 6, but suffice it to say, no one was fooled and although people were mainly very kind, I occasionally felt like a vulgar outsider, there to amuse my betters.

On the plus side, some of the senior executives wrote books on things such as how advertising worked. The amazing Jeremy Bullmore (described by *Campaign* as 'Adland's greatest philosopher') was chairman and terrified me with his intellect. There was a legendary strategist called Stephen King – not the horror writer, but equally terrifying – who had written the original book *What is a Brand?* back in 1971. Intriguingly, it said in his *Guardian* newspaper obituary many years later, 'With his immense abilities, Stephen was modest to the point of self-doubt. He once said that he felt the need to re-invent himself every seven years in case he was found out.'[1]

He was a god in his field at the time, but the quote in his obituary goes to show that everyone has insecurities, whoever we are and whatever people might think of us.

I found myself intrigued by the especially clever people called planners. They assembled in an ivory tower-type area like 'the special chosen people' and had conversations about consumer psychology, about how successful communications were about what people *took* from the message, rather than what you literally said. This was a bit of a revelation.

Better still, the job was about writing papers, doing customer analysis, being a smart presenter. Desperate to rid myself of the organizational administration that I found both boring and stressful in my client management role, I asked to transfer to the planning team. I wasn't necessarily viewed as the right stuff by the department head, but he grudgingly agreed to take me on trial; however, every fibre of his being suggested he was doing it under sufferance.

Sometimes, it can be very useful to use rejection as a drive. The importance of niceness aside, there is still something satisfying about the 'up yours' sentiment when you throw yourself into moving on.

In a bit of a huff at his grudge, I decided to look for equivalent roles in other ad agencies, and ended up at Saatchi & Saatchi again. Yes, despite my slightly difficult previous departure from there, they had a great job available in a new team and I reinvented myself in a new and smarter strategy guise.

My take-outs from this stage of my working life?

a Don't be reduced by rejection – use the power of anger in a positive way.

b Use all experiences to develop yourself in some way; you've got to try stretching yourself, even if it's to find out that you're basically OK with the core you.

c Find something you're good at and really interested in.

d Your role could be at any interesting company that seems to fit you.

Vision things

Saatchi's 'fitted' me in that second manifestation. I found my stride advising companies like Procter & Gamble, Cadbury Schweppes (now Mondelez), British Airways, BP, British Telecom, even the British Army.

It was an exciting time when British organizations were discovering a new confidence and ambition on a global stage. As a strategist and a planner, I loved being able to help them understand how they could affect their customers and audiences to help them succeed.

The 'nothing is impossible' Saatchi philosophy also permeated the culture, and I met (and later hired) some of the most extraordinary talents. I blossomed in lots of ways, although one early blossoming was a bit of a surprise. Within nine months of re-starting at Saatchi's, I discovered I was pregnant.

Best-laid plans...

In those days, you generally had to have worked for a company for a longer period to qualify for official maternity leave pay and benefits.

A bit of a worry, to say the least, and thank goodness the working world has become much more enlightened.

Fortunately, I had performed well up until that point, and I had a very supportive female department head who was philosophical about the coming event. This was in contrast to another senior woman in the media department who found she was pregnant soon after me. Her male boss threw a tantrum and threatened to sack her on the spot. This was 1987. She survived after some stern legal words to her boss. He left fairly soon after.

I managed to get offered a pretty decent maternity arrangement for those days. 'Decent' then, by the way, meant that you could actually wait until the placenta had arrived before returning to work. Just kidding of course. I had all of 10 weeks off, punctuated by business calls, but that was because my own feelings of obligation made me feel I should get back to my post as soon as I could. I would make different decisions now.

The maternity negotiation was helped by the coincidence that I had just been offered a great job as a strategist by Ogilvy & Mather (O&M), another leading ad agency. To their credit, O&M said it didn't matter, that my offer still stood, and that the MD would write to me giving me the assurance that they were totally committed to supporting my maternity leave. Which he did. What a great bunch, and a great culture. Despite the fact that I eventually decided to stay at Saatchi's for a whole number of reasons, I have never forgotten the generosity and enlightenment of O&M and have wished them well ever since, as well as recommending them to lots of people.

Guilty secrets

When I returned to work, just 10 weeks after what turned out to be a traumatic birth, let's just say I didn't feel quite my business self for a while. However, I felt a pressure to pretend that nothing had changed, that, 'Oh yeah, I had a baby yesterday, no big deal' should be the attitude. I was the first woman of any seniority to go on maternity leave and come back full-time, and I felt a big sense of responsibility. And to keep on being considered for senior roles, I felt I had to be seen as hard-working and 'present' as my male colleagues.

Whilst I never considered not going back to work, probably due to my own family experience and being absolutely determined to be financially secure and independent, dragging myself away from my small baby was honestly torture. Neither my nor my partner's long-hour jobs allowed for the flexibility to pick up from a nursery, there were no crèches near work (and frankly, taking a baby and all the equipment needed into the centre of London in the rush hour? Were we mad?), my mother was miles away and hardly able to cope with herself and partner, let alone any children, so some kind of nanny it had to be. It was difficult to afford but needs must.

BOOHOO ON CHILDCARE

One observation I have about all kinds of childcare is making sure that you apply your good management techniques to the people who help keep your life going. The childcare supervisors, nursery nurses, the teachers, the nannies and all. It seems obvious, but I could never understand why someone who was controlled and professional at work would then go home and let off their inner demons at whoever was looking after their children. They're looking after your children, for goodness' sake! If ever there were some people to be nice to, those are they! But, of course, guilt, anxiety and exhaustion can burst out in inappropriate ways. From time to time, I thought I might explode with trying to manage frustration and emotions at home; it felt like having to 'be on best management behaviour 24/7'. Needless to say, the only person who really got it in the neck was my poor long-suffering partner. Or myself. So many women have many more challenges trying to deal with complicated and/or expensive childcare, and we all need to keep fighting the good fight for quality and imaginative provision – whether at new types of workplaces or more flexible working practices shared fairly between men and women. It's a never-ending story.

If there is any happy ending to this prolonged period of pretence, exhaustion, and guilt as I struggled to be an amazing executive, mother and lover, it is this: one woman in my team later told me that, as a result of me having children as a senior department leader, it never occurred to her that she couldn't combine work and family. She ended up running a major agency group as CEO, and was incredibly supportive of other women. And at least now there is much more understanding, more time, more acknowledgement that it's not just the woman who has to try and 'do it all'.

The other happy ending is that, years later, when my children could no longer be described as children and could have a sensible conversation, they both said in different ways that they were proud of what I had achieved, and actually felt they had a lovely childhood. I tried not to take it too personally that I wasn't there a lot of the time in that childhood! However, we were really fortunate to find – and with our combined salaries, able to afford – some truly lovely nannies, who became like an extended family. I'm proud to say they are still in touch.

Having said that, my partner and I always had terrific holidays and weekends just by ourselves with the children when I could be totally devoted to them. I do hope that as long as your children know that you love them unconditionally, a lot of other life stuff is manageable.

Overall, at this point, the combination of role change to strategist (I was good at it!), the culture of Saatchi's (go for it!), and motherhood (it really *is* it!) was what provided my main foundations for greater success at work and life in the future. It undoubtedly helped that I had a supportive soulmate as a partner. The man whom I met at Saatchi & Saatchi was very much still there, although he would ruefully complain sometimes that the stored numbers on my phone were, in this order: home/the nanny; the office/ my PA; him.

First ideas about personal branding

Apart from vaulting ambition and bold creative thinking, something else I observed at Saatchi was the importance of personal branding. I didn't call it that at the time, and I doubt that many others would either, but it started to sink in that developing a distinctive personal style and perspective was important to getting on.

Maurice and Charles Saatchi, the famous founder brothers, were interesting examples of this. Maurice was billed as The Intellectual One, The Business Mind, The One Who Wore Big Glasses. These were his trademarks. He also had a wardrobe of identical white shirts and dark suits, which gave him an air of cool, smartness and control. In contrast, Charles was The Mad Creative One, The One With Wild Hair, and a reputation for shouting and throwing things, but a brilliant creative and driving force.

They assiduously managed their image, and that of the business as a uniquely ambitious and visionary brand in its own right. *Campaign* magazine (the ad industry magazine) was reduced to using the same photo of the brothers for years. Charles cultivated a super-secret persona, never meeting clients but feared and admired from afar.

I began to think more about what I wore – what that might say about me, and the impact it might have. It wasn't a huge hardship, since I always liked clothes, I had just never been able to afford very many. As I became more senior, I was able to acquire a few better pieces, and it did give me a bit more confidence.

WHAT TO WEAR?

I remember the first quite expensive designer jacket I bought when on holiday in Italy. We had a couple of hours to spare poking around the shops. I am blessed with a (now) husband who quite likes clothes and has a decent eye. I put the jacket on and it was a revelation in fit, button quality and confidence-boosting. From that moment onwards, I got jacket-itis. I have also recently moved on to 'dress-itis'. I always felt that it was good to have an interesting feature of some kind (colour, shape, an interesting slash here and there) so you don't fall into the conventional corporate uniform department.

Many people would like to believe that all this stuff shouldn't matter.

All I can say is that you would never advise a client or business owner that it's fine to put their terrific new product on a supermarket shelf in a battered, scruffy old package and hope for the best. Your appearance should reflect and do justice to the level of quality and professionalism of your work with some added distinctive touches to reflect your personality and style.

This does apply across the gender spectrum, by the way, even if it shows up in different ways. I have known just as many men of all ages who didn't present themselves in their best light. The main difference is that women still tend to have more elements to manage and, of course, to be judged by – clothing options, colours, shapes, more hair, probably more make-up. I know we're all working on the inequality of this.

By the time I got to Saatchi, I wasn't trying to pretend to be posh, overly academic or intellectual. I could be a bit racy, a bit unconventional in the way I dressed. It was very liberating. And it became an enjoyable trademark. It's good to stand out a bit, although ideally for the right reasons.

Branding yours truly

I also remember one of the early books about *Branding Yourself*,[2] which was written by a woman who used to 'do your colours' – ie to help people understand which colours either flatter or flatten your features. It was all the rage in the 1990s, when a British MP called Barbara Follett helped transform the UK Labour party front bench and made them look presentable and electable. Despite their initial disdain for such superficialities on what they looked like, enough MPs became 'Folletted' that people began to notice.

I became intrigued enough to shell out £60 for a session. It was honestly one of the best investments I made in my appearance, when I finally saw why a particular brown suit that looked great on the hanger always made me look knackered and pre-menstrual when I put it on. It's about the tone, see, and people split into those who look better with 'warm' colours, and others with the 'cool' end of the colour spectrum. Sounds mad, but just try it. It cuts your wardrobe choices to more manageable options, and you need never look like you've had a night out on the tiles again. Unless you have.

Apart from colours, I'm afraid those clichés about dressing for the job you want versus the one you have, are mainly true. It's about understanding how people make judgements and decisions. If you want to get as much influence, be as valued and valuable as you can be, you need to think about yourself in a brand-type way.

The real thing about branding

The way I look at branding is as an organizing idea for businesses and institutions as well as people. It's about how you do everything in a way that's distinctive and adds long-term value beyond day-to-day process and cost. This can apply to human beings as well as organizations. We all want to be as valued and influential as we can be, and for as long as we can.

Clearly, a lot of people can get hung up on the visible bit of the 'brand iceberg' – ie the bit you can see above the surface. The brand name, the packaging, the adverts and so on; for 'human' brands, that's the equivalent of name, personal presentation, clothes and so on. Whilst it's obviously a good idea for these 'visible' bits to be presented in a way that does justice to what lies beneath, in the long term it's the substance that counts. Your values, skills, knowledge and ambition.

Even that *Branding Yourself* book had a subtitle of *How to look, sound and behave your way to success*. The author grasped the fact that branding is as much about what you do and what you know as how you look.

That tends to mean, don't say that you want to be MD if you're not prepared to learn the mechanics about running a business. Don't say that you want to be in the boardroom if you're not prepared to learn the language of finance (that's currently the language of the boardroom, which you should grasp even if you might want to change priorities in the future). Be prepared to keep on renewing your skills and knowledge at all ages – because it's always good to try and look as though you're keeping up with the pace of technology and life as time goes on.

A BIT OF PERSONAL BRAND 101

Strong brands in any sector need three things:

1 **Clarity** – what they stand for.

2 **Coherence** – how that shows up through everything they do, say and know.

3 **Leadership** – that's both about who runs the organization, and how they symbolize the best values, but also about innovation, about restlessness and renewal.

All of these traits can be helpfully applied to building your personal brand.

Are you *clear* about what matters to you and what you're particularly good at? You don't have to know whether you want to be CEO of X Corporation by the time you're 35, and you may well need to be prepared to compromise on short-term roles to discover more about yourself, although living a lie long term is damaging.

Are you presenting, behaving and developing yourself in a way that's *coherent* with what you want? Yes, think about

---

how you look and how that builds a compelling manifestation of who you are. As far as your skills and knowledge are concerned, take courses, role-model and stretch yourself to help live up to your potential.

And *lead* your own brand by regularly challenging yourself on whether you're happy, content, learning, staying alert. Be nosey about what's happening in the world and technology. Keep your gaze up for the future as well as down on the current role.

If all that sounds exhausting… then it can be. I am saying all this with the benefit of looking in the rear-view mirror, and I still give myself a hard time. But of course, it depends on what you want to do in life, and what you'll be satisfied with. There are very few jobs that pay decently and well, or that have real influence and impact, and that are stress- and effort-free. You might as well make the most of it.

Beat yourself up. But do it in a good way.

Getting it all done

Incidentally, as far as 'giving off the right vibes' and branding yourself is concerned, don't ever let anyone think that being disorganized is somehow cute and creative.

It's not. It's a pain in the backside for you and all concerned. I know, because by nature I am that person. Let me count that ways in which it has come back to haunt me:

a   constantly worrying about dropping balls, including lying awake at night terrified you've forgotten something;

b   client contact reports/meeting minutes that you put off doing and then struggled to remember what was said;

c contracts that you delayed sending and then had to sneak in a date change to cover yourself – or having to grovel with apologies;

d likewise, approvals on anything that involved money and general perceptions of administrative incompetence;

e not briefing people in time to produce data, presentations or copy to meet deadlines, so you have to beg them to help you.

This is a moment where you may well feel smug that you are super-organized, always give people plenty of notice and never, ever miss deadlines.

You may well highlight things in different colours in your schedule according to whether they're to be done today, tomorrow, or according to a level of strategic importance.

Your inbox is streamlined, actionable and set out in a way that makes complete sense.

Your Slack is equally tight and attended.

I salute you.

You may also be the sort of person who spends so long crafting and highlighting elegant project plans that you forget you have to do something to make them happen. I was always struck by how many people seemed to think that writing an e-mail or a document was tantamount to it being done. Sadly, human behaviour isn't an automated response.

All I can say is that it took me a long time and a lot of stress (and a patronizing but effective Personal Efficiency Programme course. Summary of advice. Do it Now! Worst First! Speed Stuns! You know it makes sense...) to get it through to me that procrastination only makes things worse, that it's a good idea to keep lists and little black books. All this can be done digitally now, and there are some great apps and online efficiency tools. However, ever since I had a critical list of Reminders disappear from my iPhone, I have learned to love the physical – god bless those little Moleskine books – again.

Below are my top tips about being organized and being as effective as you can be. But I also want to admit that this is always going to be a work in progress for some. One of the many studies about Imposter characteristics suggests that procrastination is a common symptom.[3] Even after so many years in business, these are as much notes to myself as they are advice to readers:

a   Round up all the projects and tasks from all your sources in one place.

b   Spend a few minutes thinking about which are most urgent and/or important. Star them, or put them in CAPS.

c   Break them into bite-sized action chunks.

d   Get on and do them. Just get going. Even just to send a note asking someone for more information. Before you go to the bathroom, or make tea/coffee, or do that 'vital' online order/social chat.

e   Get on and do them. NOW. Prioritizing the ones you dread first.

f   Get on and do some more.

g   Feel better. And then get involved in whatever distraction you were thinking of before, but guilt-free.

h Keep adding to the main list, particularly at the end of the day. Keep on doing them.

This is all still slightly unfinished business for me, and I still manage to find myself in the adult equivalent of essay crises from time to time. But unlike most self-help books that tell you to focus solely on your bliss/accentuate the positives, I believe you also need to keep on working on your weaknesses until your dotage. Get that rod out.

NOTES TO SELF

- Try to view mistakes – personal or professional – as 'learning experiences'. Don't dwell unless it's useful therapy.

- Use rejection as an 'up yours' drive. It can be a good propeller.

- (Proper) brand thinking can be seriously helpful for you personally as well as your organization. That's as much about skills and behaviour as appearance.

- Get yourself organized. Get things done. Keep on working on yourself.

CHAPTER THREE

Hairy moments and happier outcomes

On the strangely positive power of mortification

I'm going to be covering two meanings of 'hairy' in this chapter. Both literal and symbolic, dictionary and slang. These include some personal experiences about how hair has affected me, and also about the more general, hairy scary moments in working life that can happen to anyone and that have the capacity to derail you or reduce you if you're not careful.

The thing they have in common is that both can cause mortification, and can also be managed without driving you mad.

'Hair is everything. We wish it wasn't so we could actually think about something else occasionally. But it is. It's the difference between a good day and a bad day.' This quote is from the multi-award-winning comedy-drama series *Fleabag*. It aired on the BBC and Amazon Prime from 2016, and is the story of a smart but conflicted young woman living in London. I completely loved it. It is littered with laugh-out-loud as well as poignant moments, and one of those moments is in a hairdressing salon scene. Fleabag's sister is mortified by a weird 'pencil' haircut she has just experienced, and they march back into the salon to complain. In his defence, Anthony, the stylist, eventually retorts, 'Hair isn't everything' and then Fleabag launches into the above sermon about how it actually is. You may or may not feel that strongly.

It made me howl for a number of reasons, not least of which is that mentions of bad hair days can sometimes be met with eye rolls and even crossness along the lines of 'that's so superficial/haven't we moved beyond these fripperies', particularly in group situations. But both hard research data and honest intimacies reflect the Fleabag world view. In one-on-one conversations, the truth often emerges.

Hair is indeed something that has taken on a life of its own for me, both symbolically and practically.

I am not going to be talking about the intricacies of styling here, but rather to reflect on the potential day-in, day-out distractions of our supposed crowning glory, and its impact on feelings and prospects. Again, this isn't just my view. Apparently, some 80 per cent of women admit that their hair influences their mood.[1]

Even though studies show how much men are affected by their own hair issues, they also confirm that hair seems to impact women more than men. That is usually biology as well as custom. Women tend to have more hair than men, so more can go wrong as well as right. On a more sombre note, studies show that women feel disproportionately more impacted by hair loss than men.[2]

It's significant, whichever way one looks at it.

Bad hair days

Throughout my childhood, I always had really long hair, past my waist. I cried a river during hair brushing, put up with sleeping with my hair in rags for dancing competitions, did the usual teenage 'experimentation' that made my mum cry, and then had various shades of temporary hair colours over the years, including a stint as an unlikely sun-bleached blonde when I lived in Greece in the early '80s.

But my crowning achievement in the what-was-I-thinking stakes was the henna bubble perm in the mid-'80s. Yes, I know everyone was doing it, but that's like saying it's OK for all those lemmings to leap off a cliff together.

It was particularly bad for me, because it coincided with my fish-out-of-water time at the classy and elegant J Walter Thompson agency. You could almost see lips curl at the sheer tastelessness. But the crowning moment was when a very important client said, in passing, that I had 'gypsy hair'. This was obviously in social prehistory before people rightly insisted on socially inclusive language. It was a thoroughly inappropriate but, for him, casual expression to signal that, frankly, I looked a mess. And in a coded way, that it would get in my way of getting on.

Obviously, at the time they are made, remarks like this are hurtful, and they tend to stay in your mind if you're at all self-critical. But they can also be useful galvanizers if you use them in the right way. You might occasionally feel that you want to smash something when being given 'feedback', and such personal comments are not acceptable, but I can honestly say that these difficult moments have usually helped provide a rocket for progressing in some way.

So, hurt though I was, looking in the mirror I had to admit he had a point – about the mess, anyway. I decided to stop sulking, swallowed my temptation to cut off my nose to spite my hair, and accepted the hint. I dispensed with the inappropriate bubbles of hair, lost the weird henna shades, and found that the 'hazel brown' replacement didn't speak before I did when I entered a room.

Now, I know some people may be thinking 'stuff them, just stuff them', and clearly, styles and standards move on with the decades and mores. However, I didn't feel so strongly about the loud red mess of my hair that I was prepared to let it get in the way of my career. I'm absolutely not saying you've got to change yourself to get ahead, but rather to reflect on the annoying reality of the human condition: which is that other human beings are always going to be affected by the way you present yourself.

This is even the case in places like Silicon Valley, by the way. One female CEO recently described how she felt she needed to change her hair colour from blonde to brunette to be taken as seriously as she wanted and needed when raising venture capital. She got a lot of flack for that, but says it worked for her.[3]

YOU TALKING TO ME?

When thinking about your own brand, start thinking about who you're talking to. What do you want and need them to think and possibly 'buy' from you, or be influenced by you?

Start where people are – eg if they're senior people in a formal organization and looking at you as a potential ally with their senior management or board, then they need to feel you'd make a great impression, that you'd enhance their reputation.

If, of course, you're happy to be seen as a 'creative Johnny/Jenny', or a maverick/bohemian outsider, then fine. This is sometimes useful but only if: a) you're not interested in joining boards; or b) you're already so senior, so well known and so, well, cool, that you can set the agenda and not worry about everyone else. Examples of these include the late Karl Lagerfeld, Vivienne Westwood and Richard Branson.

The rule of thumb is that, whatever you decide is right for you and what you're trying to do in life and work, it needs to look appropriate and as though you are in control of yourself and your agenda.

It helps for hair to help

Of course, there are exceptions. I remember with a dose of guilt that, when I was replacing a senior woman on a board, another board member explained that this woman had been an exceptionally high-powered and successful investment banker. That in itself made me feel suitably lowbrow. She had risen to the top in a very male-dominated business, ahead of any of the current debates about the importance of diversity and women in the boardroom. This woman had five children. I was clearly a slacker in the children production department, and it made my two look very paltry. The only thing that this board member could tell me about where the female investment banker had 'fallen short' is that she had rather 'messy hair'. A strange and ridiculous thing to mention, but in a strange and ridiculous way, reassuring to know that nobody's perfect.

In general, it's fine for someone like the wonderful Dame Mary Beard, Professor of Classics at Newnham College, Cambridge, to have slightly eccentric hair (although even Mary confesses to loving shoes). But looking like a unique English academic is an intrinsic part of her personal brand. And she's a one-off.

If you're trying to look like you can run something professionally and efficiently, looking like you can't even run your hair is quite something to get over for most people in business.

I must also confess that, apart from the red and radical period, I have had many other times where my hair has not been my best asset.

Particularly when the children were small, I was working full-time and felt shattered a lot of the time. Not only was I time-poor, but the cost of childcare, mortgages and general life meant that I got into a thrift habit of dyeing my hair myself and only having the occasional professional cut.

I will call this my Morticia Adams phase, as my hair got progressively blacker, and more matte, under the plaque build-up of cheap dyes. I felt I needed to colour my hair because genetics meant I started to go grey early. Not to mention the effect of stress. That's not to say you can't look amazing with pepper and salt or pure white hair in your 30s, but I just didn't like it on me.

It was only years later and after some serious remedial work with a leading colourist that I realized what a huge difference the hair colour thing could make. I saw a picture of the actor and model Liz Hurley in a magazine, decided that I'd like to have a few honey-coloured highlights like she did, and called the salon mentioned in the editorial. The resulting hairdresser relationship has endured through thick and thin.

I bumped into someone I used to work with several years before and they said, 'Wow, you look much younger than when I last saw you'. I am sure they meant well, but the way they said it suggested that they thought I had looked rubbish the last time, and that I had perhaps 'had some work done'. I hadn't, but the hair colour was clearly more flattering. It probably also helped that my children were at an almost human stage by that time and I was getting some sleep.

Clearly, when you are younger, you can get away with a bit more because of natural youthful beauty and sheen, and the dazzle can compensate for less disposable income for hair, make-up and clothes. Even so, it helps to give it a bit of thought.

When your hair blows you away

These days, I find a weekly blow dry a bit of an addiction as well as indulgence. I particularly find it difficult to do those back bits myself. The loudest I ever laughed at a Harry Potter film was when Hermione was watching herself in the past in *Harry Potter and the Prisoner of Azkaban*. She was with Harry and Ron in a different time dimension. All very philosophical and important stuff for the plot, and the three school friends were meant to be discussing their plan to win the day, but the first thing Hermione said was, 'Is that *really* what my hair looks like from the back?'

I am also grateful that dry shampoo has come back into my life in so many forms. When I was a teenager, dry shampoo was (almost literally) a bit of a dirty secret. Whereas now, dry shampoo is a styling aid! A fragrant refresher! An indispensable part of hair maintenance for the modern woman! I think that's what's called great brand renewal... .

I have always looked with envy at those women who never seem to have a flaw, who are constantly plucked, trimmed and swishy in the right places. You can overcome, but you don't half have to compensate. The important thing is to have some saving graces, make an effort in all the ways you can (so you don't look like you don't care at all or can't get it together at all) and have a sense of self-deprecating humour about the other stuff.

TOP-OF-HEAD SUGGESTIONS

1 If you see something/someone you like in terms of hair styles, copy it. This is so much easier today with social media.

2 It's obviously all down to personal taste, but it's just worth thinking about what you'd like this rather visible aspect of personal presentation to say about you, and to make you feel.

3 If you have smart or tailored clothes, you can always go for a less structured formal hairstyle. If you prefer more casual clothes, perhaps balance this with more orderly hair. It's just a view.

4 Batiste *Dry Shampoo* is a special friend.

And now for the other meaning of hairy...

There are moments in all our working lives which can euphemistically be described as 'intense learning moments', when things go horribly wrong. They are mortifying at the time, but hopefully won't kill you and will indeed make you stronger.

After you've spent the first year or so in your job thinking, 'Ooh, this is great being with interesting people and helping out... and I'm getting paid for it!', there comes a moment when you realize you're actually going to have to be accountable. That means that if there's a mistake in a piece of public communication, a spelling mistake in an e-mail that accidentally changes the meaning or you forget to do something to a deadline, then it's, Yes, Your Personal Fault. And it could cost the company money, lose a client or their trust, or at the very least you could get an unwelcome piece of 'feedback'.

This feeling of 'I need to worry about this' never goes away, in any role, or at any level. It applies whether you are in a big company, a start-up or any industry. Jobs where there's really no stress just don't exist. If you were ever thinking about dropping out, even doing a bit of subsistence farming and living 'off-grid', this also has big stresses and strains. I'm thinking weather, mud, and creepy crawlies. Or worse. Honestly, there's no escape, and the issue is how you deal with stress and manage the inevitable screw-ups.

FEELING ON TOP OF STUFF EVEN WHEN YOU'RE NOT

- A deliberate choice of wardrobe that gives you the confidence that at least you look the part.

- A decent notebook for taking notes and keeping thoughts in one place, or perhaps an app like Notability. I know some people don't think that leaders should be seen taking a lot of notes, but personally I have a memory like a sieve and needs must.

- A confident posture, conscious breathing and a steady gaze are all things you can use to help you with gravitas. More detail about this in the 'Voices Off' chapter.

I have a few particular examples of awfulness in meetings which still haunt me, and from which I certainly learned a few lessons. Mistakes are a necessary rite of passage. And very human.

Letting the side down

Maurice Saatchi (Lord Saatchi himself) once asked me to look after something for him quite early in my career. It was to do some research for one of his high-powered business friends, to help them prove the effectiveness of their technology publishing business. I thought I did the right things – identifying someone from a research company within the group who seemed to know what he was talking about, briefing them, agreeing the cost with the client and so on.

The researcher actually looked like a central casting academic with beard, tweed jacket and thick glasses. This was obviously not a problem in itself, but he did look a bit out of place with these high-powered technology people, who just wanted a clear and practical set of insights. He duly did the fieldwork, mentioned in passing that there had been one or two challenges but that there were interesting findings. I should have spotted that red flag.

I fixed the de-brief date with the client, was very busy on other projects in the meantime, then showed up to the meeting, having not actually seen the presentation myself. I imagined myself as the facilitator, the convener, rather than the person responsible for the work.

The first words the client said in a pleasant and positive tone were, 'Well, we're looking forward to this, and getting a clear steer!'

The researcher looked slightly embarrassed, shuffled his papers and cleared his throat and said, 'Well, actually, no,

I'm afraid I can't say there's a clear result you can use, and there was a problem with the sample…'.

I broke out into a cold sweat as the client's face turned to red thunder… and to me, as (in his view) the responsible party.

'What do you mean, there's no clear result? You mean, you've taken our money and this research is useless?'

Oh my god, I'm thinking. It's for Maurice! I've well and truly screwed up! My career is over, and other such happy thoughts.

The meeting could have stopped there, but fortunately the researcher, having delivered the opening bombshell, then started saying that there were still some interesting findings, even if not what the client had actually asked for.

The meeting shuffled forward, just about getting back on speaking terms, but you could have cut the atmosphere with a knife and it was clear that the client was fighting to keep his temper under control. The goodbyes were a little stiff to say the least.

He maybe calmed down a little, because I didn't get my marching orders that day. But Maurice Saatchi had a wonderful way not only of making you feel great if you'd done a good job, but also of making sure that you knew if you hadn't. He mentioned in passing later that he 'gathered there had been some problems with the research'.

His quiet disappointment was a much more powerful drive to improve than having someone ranting, which tends to make people panic into stupidity or creates an opponent who seeks to get their own back in some way in the future.

MAKING ASSUMPTIONS

Here's what I learned, which might be more generally applicable:

- Never assume.

- Never assume that someone has done exactly what you thought or wanted until you have seen it.

- Never assume that technology is going to work unless you have checked it beforehand.

- Never surprise people in a bad way, and particularly not in front of others when they were supposed to know what's happening.

- Confess to mistakes in a timely way.

- Make sure you have thought of a solution to the problem and what you're going to do about it. This could include: waiving the cost, being generous in an offer of further work, and good service recovery generally. Going above and beyond to compensate can be an excellent route to building greater trust at a later date.

- If, at some point, you want to help someone else improve their performance, it tends to be more effective for people to feel they may have disappointed you, rather than be on the receiving end of deranged shouting.

Years later, I got to know the client in a different context, and as a fellow senior executive as opposed to the client–agency power imbalance. When I confessed how worried I had been about the incident, he expressed real surprise that it was such a big thing for me when he hardly remembered it. He said he was cross with people all the time, and that this had been very mild by comparison.

It gets worse...

But the hairy 'take the biscuit' bad experience was undoubtedly a business meeting with a certain high-profile and multimillionaire business person.

I occasionally used to bump into him at industry drinks receptions. We sometimes exchanged a few words (or rather, I blathered nervously) but I always got the impression that there were always many and much more important people he wanted to talk to. Probably because there always were.

Having read about some of this person's business challenges, I thought I'd drop him a line as a piece of new business prospecting. To my surprise and delight (or so I thought), he called the next day, said he'd like to meet, and we fixed a time. My team did quite a lot of prep work for the meeting and developed a few ideas.

However, I made the mistake of not doing enough research on him, or what he was really like to deal with in business, and what he might be expecting or looking for (that 'never assume' rule again).

We were ushered up to his suitably enormous office and I felt unusually intimidated and nervous.

And boy, did it show as I stumbled over my words. I allowed myself to be thoroughly put off by his constant, aggressive pushbacks. That was, as I should have found out, his usual style. I knew what I wanted to say, but it didn't come across that way.

At one point, he turned to his sidekick and said, 'Well, I don't know what she's on about, do you?'

The sidekick side-kicked nervously, 'No, no, no, I don't'.

I think he was trying to be funny, but it was humiliating and upsetting, and all the more so because it was such a wasted effort.

So, what did I learn from this experience?

a Do your homework on the client, their style and their business culture, just as much as you would do on the business challenges themselves.

b Prepare and rehearse for what could be challenges and objections.

c Don't allow yourself to look so nervous. More practical tips on how to do this in the 'Voices Off' chapter.

And what I wanted to say to the difficult client?

a If you want the best from people, it's best not to intimidate them.

b Meetings don't have to be a show of macho strength.

c If you are not nice to people, they will eventually want to get their own back.

'Who are you?' and other social gaffes

I was once at a high-powered business party, and got introduced to someone called Tom, whom I thought I vaguely recognized. We chatted about how we knew the hosts, where we lived and so on, and I got around to asking what he did.

'I write', he said.

'Oh, that's interesting', I replied.

At that moment, someone butted into our 'conversation' and took him away. I asked someone else who Tom was. They looked at me as though I had just crawled out from under a stone.

'That's Tom Stoppard.'

Let's just say it was my Notting Hill/Julia Roberts film moment. I committed the cardinal sin of not recognizing the UK's greatest living playwright, at a sophisticated party. It's good to keep working on your memory, at any age and stage.

A CASE OF FORGOTTEN IDENTITY

It's also good to remember that you should never feel pleased with yourself at any age and stage of life and career, nor take for granted that anyone might take notice of you just because you have been around for a while.

I had met a well-respected business titan on a number of occasions, at business drinks receptions, business friends' parties and dinners.

I have actually had quite long conversations with him.

I have sat on a conference panel (of only three people) with him, discussing 'the new consumer'.

On that panel, he even said, 'I agree with Rita'.

More recently, I have twice seen him at functions and said hello.

The second time he gave me such a 'no idea who you are' look, I even helped him in a slightly faltering voice, 'Er, it's Rita Clifton…'.

Still absolutely no flicker of recognition.

I was tempted to give him my own 'keep working on the memory' advice.

Sometimes, though, you've just got to suck up your own insignificance.

I have no leg to stand on in calling out others, even though it's NEVER intentional.

Here are a couple more examples of me wanting the ground to open and swallow me up.

We were pitching for a huge account.

I picked up the client from reception and was chatting about how we prided ourselves in great relationships within teams etc, and that we aimed to achieve almost a modern family feel.

We arrive in the room and I start to introduce people. We get to the design director and I suddenly froze in fear.

My mind was blank. Totally blank.

I tried to rack my brain and visualize the team photo line-up. I tried to replay a previous conversation with them, like silently singing through song lyrics to try and remember the title, hoping the name would just fall into place.

But it was too late.

I was even reduced to using the colloquial 'haha, senior moment' line, but the damage was done.

What impact did I think this had? The client thought I was lying about the close working culture, the designer was upset and trying to be brave and laugh about it. It was an excruciating start. We didn't get the brief, and the designer left soon afterwards.

I can only ask their forgiveness and try not to let it happen again.

What I learned from this, even after many years in business, was this: if you have ANY problems remembering names, NEVER, NEVER set yourself up to do introductions. Preferably, get people to introduce themselves. Hopefully, they'll remember who they are.

And it's good to keep on beating yourself up to be better – there are many tips and tricks to remember people's names. For example, repeat their name while looking straight at them, and use it some more times in the conversation. Concentrate. Associate their name and face with someone or something you know, like if someone is called George and is a lawyer, think about George and Amal Clooney in your mind's eye. Never underestimate how forgetting people's names and stories can upset them and trigger their own imposter feelings. Remember how it feels when done to you.

A right royal mess-up

As other difficult stories go, it was tough to beat an occasion at Buckingham Palace. I was chairing a conservation charity and we were lucky enough to have HRH the Duke of Edinburgh as Patron. I say lucky, and he was truly amazing.

We had generously been offered a reception at the Palace for volunteers, funders, sponsors and partners. The prospect of meeting Prince Philip had been a great draw and I was hopeful of getting more support for the charity.

What became very obvious very quickly was that once the Duke arrived at the event, as chair I would ideally accompany him around the room, prepared to introduce people if necessary and generally oiling social wheels.

Clearly, Prince Philip is completely practised at this type of room circulation. Not so me, and I suddenly realized that I had not prepared enough, didn't know half the people in the room, and certainly didn't have enough background on who they were, or what relationship they had (or that we wanted them to have) with the charity.

This was my fault, entirely.

As result, I had to get the charity's main organizer to be at my shoulder so that I could be at the Duke's. They muttered to me, I muttered at hopefully the right times in those conversations. I thought I was going to have a heart attack.

Final learnings from the 'who on earth are you' syndrome:

- Prepare, prepare, prepare. As though you were revising for an exam.
- Again, memorize someone's face attached to their name (even attached to a memorable image) and say it aloud a few times for it to stick.
- If you vaguely recognize people but are not sure, don't embarrass yourself by going out of your way to say, 'Don't I know you?'
- I learned from a diplomat that you always need to act as though you've met someone before (eg say things like 'good to see you', rather than 'good to meet you'), and then ask things like 'how are you spending your time at the moment?' to help give you clues, as well as conversation. You know the score.

In general, you're only as hairy as you allow yourself to be, and to feel. And just learn from the hair-raising moments. You know it makes sense.

NOTES TO SELF

- Whether we like it or not, hair and overall appearance talks.

- It's probably good to make a deliberate choice about what it says.

- Never assume anything's OK unless you've checked it.

- Learn to remember people's names, and when to stop digging.

- Whether deliberate or not, you'll always be a no one to someone.

- Learn to laugh, even if through gritted teeth.

CHAPTER FOUR

Magic numbers and difficult statistics

On why no numbers = no boardroom

In her 2006 work *Book of Numbers,* Shakuntala Devi states that:

> Many go through life afraid of numbers and upset by numbers. They would rather amble through life miscounting, miscalculating and, in general, mismanaging their worldly affairs than make friends with numbers.[1]

Likewise, Mark Twain has a lot to answer for on the whole 'lies, damned lies and statistics' front. I know he didn't actually say it himself, although he did say, 'Figures often beguile me'. It all adds up to an impression that for lofty minds, numbers are somehow suspect, an enemy of art and literature. That they are for the vulgar commercial or political classes to mystify and manipulate others.

It's so annoying when that suspicious view puts people off. Numbers can truly be your friend, and can help you radically change and improve businesses and organizations.

The first personal and practical revelation about this was when I was poking around in consumer research about who used a particular anti-dandruff shampoo; my working life has had no end of glamour. What the quantitative customer data showed was the dramatic difference in usage and attitude between those who described themselves as having 'heavy dandruff' and those who just thought they had a 'light shower'.

Basically, people imagined the brand I was looking after either contained the equivalent of battery acid to strip out the offending flakes, or a dose of superglue to keep the dandruff stuck on. Either way, only the people who thought they had a Serious Social Problem with dandruff were prepared to buy it regularly. A bit of a business limitation. The client was strangely impressed with my insights. Also the fact that I had given them numbers as evidence meant that their senior managers would listen. This revelation led to a whole new way of them looking at how to advertise the brand, and to develop new hair products that were packaged so that they didn't look like you could also use them to clean bathroom surfaces. I was strangely pleased with myself and from that moment always tried to find something interesting that numbers were showing.

But without doubt, the most influential numbers in business still have hard currency attached.

Money does indeed talk

Sometimes, I wish I had done three years of finance and accountancy when I left university. Not that I wanted to be a career accountant, but it would have been so useful to use finance as a native language to run businesses and the boardroom. I have had to learn it over time, and particularly when I became CEO at the age of 39. However, it's a bit like learning a foreign language at an older age. You'll always have a strange accent and hit some odd notes.

I say this because, whether we like it or not, a big part of the language of the boardroom is finance. And if you don't speak that language, you either won't get there, or won't make the most of being there. Chapter 5 goes into more detail about this.

Although I was decent at mathematics at school, I also suffered from the strange and inexplicable separation between arts and science in senior school (Leonardo da Vinci seemed to blend the two without agonizing over subject choices). I duly did languages at A-level and university and for a while proceeded to forget how to do any calculations other than how to scratch money together to avoid an overdraft, although this is not a useless skill.

BOYS, GIRLS AND NUMBERS

Based on a UK study, girls are apparently still not as interested in studying sciences at university as boys despite a rise in popularity of STEM (science, technology, engineering and maths) subjects at A-level.[2]

Most popular subjects for boys

1 economics;

2 law;

3 medicine;

4 computer science;

5 maths;

6 history;

7 accounting and finance;

8 mechanical engineering;

9 psychology;

10 physics.

Most popular courses for girls

1 psychology;

2 law;

3 medicine;

4 history;

5 geography;

6 criminology;

7 English;

8 midwifery;

9 architecture;

10 maths.

What's also interesting is that a different international study found that, even though girls and boys around the world had similar test scores in science subjects, by a strange paradox, the more a country had gender equality (according to the Global Gender Gap Index), the fewer girls chose science subjects and professions. There are various theories around this, including that women in less equal societies could see STEM professions as the clearest path to financial freedom.[3]

Like it or not, a lack of facility with numbers can damage your influence. If you rely on others to provide you with data, and/or if you seem allergic or uninterested in the quantitative at the expense of the qualitative, you are asking for trouble, or not to be taken seriously.

This is obviously not to say that having a passionate point of view, allied with great creativity and insights about people, humanity and the rest are not vitally important – and are particularly needed now in the world. They will get you a long way. But probably not right to the top, where you are truly controlling an organization, or your own destiny.

Keeping it real means knowing the numbers

As an example, I recall a senior colleague who was an amazing and well-rounded business person, who had been approached by a famous luxury fashion group to talk about being CEO.

This person said they might be interested, but at the time they had heard that the business was losing money. Not unreasonably, they said that they would want to meet the legendary founder to make sure that they were on board with what might need to be done to get the business back to survival and profitability.

Oh no, the other company's directors said, the founder didn't know about the financial difficulties that the business was in, and neither would they want to. They just wanted to focus on the 'creative vision'.

The fact that the creative founder had produced a series of seasons of unwearable fashion and had lost direction was off limits. All this would be understandable if the founder had been prepared to live in a garret suffering for their art but no, they wanted private planes, dedicated hotel suites and all the trappings of a luxury lifestyle.

My friend said thanks, but it wasn't for them.

Whilst they were prepared to work with the founder to get mutual trust and understanding of creative and business priorities, they were not prepared to live in la-la land. Trusting another person to manage the finances whilst you get on with the vision thing is one thing; refusal to acknowledge the importance of financial reality another. The founder lost control because they didn't want to 'lose their soul' in numbers. This was their loss, sadly.

The bottom line

You could name endless pop stars, bands and artists who have 'trusted' a manager to organize the deals and finance whilst the 'talent' gets on with the music and creation. They end up on those 'Whatever Happened To' programmes that feature celebrities who said they didn't think about money whilst spending it like, well, rock stars, until their manager told them it had all gone... having run off with a very large percentage of it themselves.

There's a reason why people like Mick Jagger (notoriously parsimonious with money) and Paul McCartney (notoriously sensible with money) have outlasted them all.

THIS IS THE BUSINESS

There are obviously quite a lot of tomes written about the key principles and practices of doing business and making money. I have found the following simple points generally useful:

a You need to be able to *sell* products and services to people for *more than it costs* to produce them (it's up to you and your business model and conscience to decide how much more).

b You need to have enough cash *in the bank* to pay people and for the things you need to do business day-to-day: a lack of cash is the main reason for businesses going under.

c You need to keep *truthful records* of what you're doing.

Finance and accounting turns the above into a planetary system and foreign language all of its own. Whether it excites you or not, you need to be able to read a balance sheet and make sense of income statements and management accounts at the very least.

There are numerous books and courses that help non-financial people with finance (various Idiot's Guides, if you prefer, as well as the more dignified FT *Finance for Non-Financial Managers* versions), and you can rehearse the difference between EBT, EBIT, EBITDA, EBITDAR, or even OIBDA. In Chapter 5, I've included a basic guide to finance-speak to get things going in case you're not already familiar. I just want to emphasize that an investment of time and effort to understand money and finance will pay career dividends on all levels. 'No finance' tends to mean 'no boardroom'.

Exposure to the hard core of business

My rude awakening happened when I first became CEO of a major brand consultancy. Whilst I sort of understood the basics of business (see above: essentially, we had to win as much business and income as we could, control costs without killing people or systems... and get clients to pay their bills), the first time my finance director said the auditors wanted to meet me, it was all I could do not to ask why. I then sat in a meeting with them while they talked about the audit happily being clean, getting good cooperation from the finance team, and that they were happy to sign off. It was only later that I fully understood why that should be so important.

Leading a business is obviously about generating and doing great business, but it's also about making sure you can show (and prove) due good process. You've got to manage any risks responsibly (like market downturns, client security, health and safety and so on), and make sure no one's cooking books and over-enthusiastically overstating how much business you're doing. Even if these areas are not the greatest interest to you personally, as a business leader you need to make sure you signal to ALL your staff that what they do in the whole *doing business thing* is important. Because it is – if you want to have enough money and have a good enough reputation to stay in business. That means having financial systems and controls that give your funders/banks confidence. And if anything goes wrong, remember, it's on YOUR watch.

The significance of hard numbers management came back to me later, when I became a FTSE non-executive director. I understood that it was fundamental to the board agenda and being legally responsible for a business so I was grateful for the familiarity.

I also remember having a meeting with the former Group CEO of the company, who had originally hired me as CEO. He had said at the time that he was aware I hadn't been an MD/CEO before, but that he believed that I could do it because of my 'other great attributes' (more later) and that, anyway, I would have an excellent finance director to help me.

That last point was only partially true, as the brilliant finance director was actually pregnant with twins and had six weeks to countdown. I was, of course, very understanding and pleased for her… but oh my god!

A month or so into the CEO role, I had another meeting with the Group CEO, where he asked me to run through the forecast. It was a few sheets of paper, packed with numbers, which showed the usual month, year to date and next few months' forecast. Out of the corner of my eye, I could see him watching me carefully as I pointed out a few things rather self-consciously, mainly focusing on the top line and new business prospects. He nodded, perfectly nicely, and then picked up his pen and proceeded to point out, yes, but look at these ratios, that marketing expenditure that I should cut back on right now if those projects don't come in or if there was a problem with that client paying bills and so on.

He had previously worked in corporate finance and I was never going to be able to compete with his natural habitat. He was, tactfully or otherwise, trying to school me in preparation for future onslaughts from the holding company.

Whether I liked it or not, I realized I would have to get it, to get interested, and with or without a good finance director by my side, the buck stopped with me. I swore then and there that I would always be prepared in future, top, bottom and all lines in between, and would try and help others be so too.

If I was honest, he was right to be a bit concerned. I could certainly do the 'lead practitioner' part of the brand consultancy CEO job and was good at new business and people management. But you've got to be on top of the numbers to be CEO, whatever business you're in.

In my previous role at Saatchi's, I had risen to vice chairman and strategy director. Whilst I was on the most senior management team and worked very closely with the CEO and CFO, my role had been as the one with the long-term customer insight and business overview. It was easy to be lofty and say things like 'that doesn't make sense for the long term/we should be investing' etc. As a strategist, you can look into dignified middle distance when people start talking money, budgets and receivables (except your own, obviously).

But as CEO, you often feel like saying, 'Forget the long term – just look at these terrible monthly figures.'

Without a well-managed short term, you might not *have* a long term. Although equally, if you don't have a long-term strategic view, short-term activity is unfocused and unlikely to build a sustainably valuable business. Holding these two parts in your mind in the right proportions is the essence of a good CEO and a successful business leader.

If you ever need some extra inspiration and cheer on the finance front, try reading some Warren Buffet, the world's most successful investor and all-round financial sage. He hasn't done too badly. And apparently, Mr Buffet spends 80 per cent of his day reading. To get into the mind of the billionaire investor there are over 300 books to choose from. His *Letters to Berkshire Hathaway Shareholders* is a good place to start.

The importance of the whole brain in business

You have probably heard about left and right brain theory, where the left side is supposedly more rational and analytical, and the right side more emotional and creative. Whilst this theory has now been questioned, there is no doubt that some people feel more comfortable with logic and method in the way they work, and others with intuition and the qualitative.

In terms of the power of analytics and numbers, firms like McKinsey show that, if you have numbers-based evidence and look Serious about Strategy, you can rule the world. McKinsey alumni crop up at the heads of so many corporations around the world.

A major reason for their influence is their rigorous, forensic analysis, through charts, numbers, scenarios and financial projections, and they look like they would keep secrets (a crucial part of their brand). They are the corporate equivalent of a security blanket.

It's worth remembering that although wholly rational analysis often sounds good in a rational boardroom, it doesn't necessarily uncover the human reality that might make the biggest difference to current and future market performance. Humans are, frankly, a bit messy, and it's not a bad idea to have slightly 'messier' people around the boardroom and senior management table (ie people who are less afraid to talk about the human stuff) to make sure that gets taken into account. They just might not get to run the company.

Business hard and soft

Online data collection and analysis has changed the game since the early days of consumer market research, and it's easier to look at the 'big data' on what people actually do, and what might have led up to them doing that without having to ask them directly. The point is that numbers (a bit like 'these results came off a computer, so they must be right') are only as good as the assumptions and factors that are put in.

I say all this because the ideal sweet spot to run the world and persuade people to make it more human needs both hard numbers and soft intuition.

In fact, strike that.

I am infuriating myself by saying that intuition is soft – a bit like saying intangible value is soft when for so many companies it is the biggest economic driver. It makes the intangible feel less important, when it may well make the biggest difference. Business practice and culture can often beat the human and intuition factor out of people.

There are a number of answers to this dilemma. One I found particularly useful was to be able to put a hard value on the so-called 'soft stuff'. The brand thing, for example. It can give you a whole new currency to win people over.

As a strategist in an ad agency (and particularly one like Saatchi's, with great access to business leaders), you get to spend a lot of time analysing consumer behaviour, and conducting focus groups to try and understand why people (think they) do and choose certain things – and what might appeal. You just have to bear in mind that what comes out of people's mouths does not necessarily represent what's going on in their heads and hearts. However, you've got to apply a bit of psychology, and indirect ways of getting at their real views (go to www.mrs.org.uk if you're interested to find out more on this stuff). You have to balance these kinds of qualitative insights with quantitative research; this latter type looks at how *many* people think or do this, where they are, their demographics and attitudes, etc, so you can build a brand and marketing strategy that works at the scale you need.

However, even if you have got quantitative consumer data to 'prove' preferences and behaviour, you've still got to connect that with business performance – particularly with the traditionally bald financial metrics about what's driving revenue and profit. And, of course, that also involves deciding how much an organization should invest in brand strategy and marketing.

High flying

I say invest, but infuriatingly and tellingly, marketing is classified as an expense rather than an investment in accounting terms.

This issue was thrown into sharp relief when I was working on the British Airways (BA) advertising account in the 1990s. At that time, BA had the highest profile and most imaginative advertising of any airline or travel business. It won lots of creative awards in that period, and all the consumer research confirmed that it made people feel that BA was the most special and interesting airline in the world. But, the 'image' advertising also committed a cardinal sin as far as short-term revenue metrics were concerned: it didn't seem to make customers leap on the planes the next week or month. That's because it tended to take them longer to plan trips and decide on destinations than buying a new toothpaste.

The fact that the advertising made people feel they'd be willing to pay a premium for BA, and that it created a virtuous circle of goodwill and recommendation, was lost. The BA finance team at the time said that the marketing budget should be radically reduced in favour of direct selling and promotions, which they could measure with precision. But there's actually a great saying attributed to John Maynard Keynes, that it's 'better to be roughly right rather than precisely wrong'. Unfortunately, that seemed to pass people by.

Out of frustration, I contacted a brand consultancy called Interbrand, which had recently pioneered something called brand valuation. This looked at the brand as an asset to a business, and calculated how much that asset was worth in hard financial terms through some clever factors that united the principles of finance and marketing.

The document they created did the rounds for two years at BA, and made a difference to how the company viewed brand marketing – not as something that was annually expensed in the income statement, but as feeding an asset that needed to be invested in (just like planes, buildings, customer data and the rest). Later, a new management regime came in and these insights were buried again. But nevertheless, a real breakthrough at the time.

In fact, this was such a breakthrough for me that I later joined Interbrand so I could take the 'brand as valuable financial asset versus flaky, softy marketing comms thing' to a lot more organizations, and to boards who made the investment decisions. This brand understanding for all businesses and boards is still a work in progress, but the hard financial connection of good branding to business has made a huge difference – and has increased people's understanding that building a brand is the best way to generate reliable, sustainable influence and value. (And the same applies to your own personal brand too. We'll come back to that one).

Meanwhile, a takeaway from this experience is that, if you find an issue, a cause, a company that gives you a huge amount of energy, seriously look at joining it and doing it.

Returning to the importance of those numbers again, there's another wryly amusing example that had a particular impact on me.

Revenge of the nerds in the ad industry

When I first worked in ad agencies, they were what you might call full-service agencies. Officially, it meant that, if a company went to an advertising agency, they would get the full works – strategy, creative work, TV, press and poster ads as well as some design and innovation – and also, a team to plan and buy the media you'd need from the media owners like TV stations, billboard companies, newspapers and magazines.

I don't think I'm betraying any secrets that there used to be a hierarchy in the agency world. Basically, the creative department were top dogs (or so they thought anyway) and felt they should be treated as such. The client management teams sort of ran the place, but only by grace of the creative teams not throwing tantrums. The strategists (of which I was one), were the ones who supposedly came up with clever research, business insights and strategies that would inspire great creative work and prove that it worked, although they often felt under-appreciated. But without doubt, the most under-appreciated and caricatured team was the media department.

They were the ones who would have the equivalent of pencils and calculators spilling out of their pockets, and often in those days, where it was permissible and even oblig-atory to smoke everywhere, the media buyers would have a cigarette hanging out of the mouth, whilst at the same time shouting and exchanging insults with the media owners to get the best deal on the advertising space. They might then make up over a long boozy lunch. More often than not, in new business pitches, the media bit would be squeezed at the end of the presentation, and I can think of several instances where the agency ran out of time whilst spending ages discussing the strategy and the creative work, and then might say dismissively, 'oh, well, the media section is in the document' – this, despite the fact that the poor media executive might have been up half the night preparing.

Roll forward 20 years, and revenge was theirs. To make the agency businesses more profitable, agency owners began to split out the creative work and media planning/buying into separate companies. And guess who got the upper hand in the power balance between creative and media?

The media teams had the numbers, the statistics, the charts, the demonstrable financial value. The creative agen-cies had the smarts, the pictures and the glamour, but lost out on the budgets and the power balance.

Not so common sense

You don't get points for being 'right' in business (or in real life generally). And, believe it or not, lots of people with different views also think THEY are right too. You only get 'points' for being able to bring someone to your point of view, by persuading them either overtly or subtly to that. Evidence helps.

In an increasingly neurotic and reputation-risk-fearing age, people need hard evidence to give them the confidence to act. Because, if you're running any kind of a commercial or a non-profit organization, whether you like it or not, you need to justify your actions and be able to defend your decisions. In today's organizational world, it's not sufficient any more even just to do what you believe is the right thing. You have to be able to give hard evidence for it, or risk being fined, fired or flattened in the media. Even then you might not be safe.

So, you can keep on shouting that it's all rubbish and rage against the numbers, or you can just use them. It's an 'and' not an 'either'. Best get over any hang-ups, at least until you get to the very top. And then see if you can change things.

Now for some sex…

There are statistics, and then there are the moments where numbers speak louder than words. What follows may be some statistics about sex, but there's nothing remotely sexy about them.

It started as a light-hearted request for me to speak at a conference about alcoholic drinks and changing consumer drinking habits. The title the organizers had given me was 'Women: the Majority Sex' and they asked me to speak about how marketing alcoholic drinks to women had changed and would change. I think they were hoping for some research on what motivated women to drink, followed by some ideas on the opportunity for better drinks marketing to women, finally followed up with some funny advertising campaigns.

My qualifications for this were that I had worked on Harveys Bristol Cream sherry at some point, and also, by way of contrast, on Castlemaine XXXX lager. (If you remember, the slogan was 'Australians wouldn't give a XXXX about anything else'.) And, my main claim to alcohol advertising fame was that I worked on some famous Babycham advertising.

You may or may not be familiar with Babycham. When I was growing up, it felt like the height of excitement at Christmas that I might eventually be grown-up enough to be offered a special, saucer-shaped champagne glass of what was then called a 'genuine champagne perry'; perry being something made of pears, in Somerset in the UK, and certainly not made in Champagne in France. However, it came in exquisite, sweet little individual bottles with a famous leaping fawn logo, and when I say sweet, the actual liquid substance almost felt like it was taking your teeth out. The legendary catchphrase in advertising was 'I'd LOVE a Babycham', usually said by a slightly simpering but attractive woman being bought a drink by a debonair guy at a bar. Magic would then happen, with the cartoon fawn leaping around and spreading cheer. After years of decline, the new brief to my agency in the mid-1980s was that they wanted to change perceptions of the brand, to a slightly older, more sophisticated audience.

The resultant advertising was pretty crass by today's standards, but it featured a busy and 'cool' bar, when a young debutante-like woman wearing pearls says, 'I'd love a Babycham'. The whole place stops and goes silent as people absorb the full social horror of someone ordering such an unfashionable drink in public. But then… a cool-looking guy wearing sunglasses clicks his fingers, and says, 'Heh, *I'd* love a Babycham'. Then, crowds of cool trendy people rush to the bar clamouring for the golden, fizzy, peary liquid. You get the picture. The profile went up like a firework, sales soared, and I found myself being asked to speak at conferences.

And now for the real thing...

But when I was preparing my presentation for the drinks conference, I was having a think about the 'Majority Sex' title, and how to play it. Being a geeky strategist, I looked at the premise, and duly researched the percentage of women in the population. In the UK, and all industrially developed nations, it was true that women were in the majority. But actually, that was only because they tended to live longer; there were so many examples of older women living as widows, not having married by choice or indeed, never having married if they were unlucky about timing and losing a generation of young men in the world wars. Lower down the age range, gender split numbers were pretty equal.

I then began to realize the full horror of the statistics elsewhere. In countries like China, India and the Middle East, men were significantly in the majority. There were a number of causes, but some key factors were gender-related early abortion, female infanticide, women dying in childbirth or not getting the right medical help.

There was, and still is, a marked cultural, social and economic preference for boys and males in some societies. In China, around 119 boys are born for every 100 girls (and in India this figure is 115 boys born for every 100 girls, with economists projecting there may be as many as 30–40 million more men of marriageable age in both countries by 2020).[4] There are some villages in China where there are no females at all. This imbalance is so severe that it is in danger of creating huge social unrest and potential civic violence as young men with few prospects, either of jobs or of partners, make their presence felt. And yes, I know that Russia swings the other way on male/female gender balance as men tend to die young, often from alcohol-related illnesses.

As far as the drinks conference was concerned, I must confess that I slightly lost my sense of humour. I did my best, but suddenly, loving a Babycham wasn't quite so appealing. I stopped seeing sex(-ual equality) as a light and funny subject, and started feeling angry. It's been difficult to stop it since then, even though raw anger is best moderated for day-to-day life.

For everyone who thinks that we 'go too far' in trying to address the power, pay and social balance between men and women in the developed world, well, there's a whole other world out there that needs some radical help. Showing what a truly equal, balanced and civilized society can do as an exemplar must be the way to go.

On a parochial level, what's disappointing is that men still dominate senior positions in supposedly 'enlightened' industries as well. Ironically, whereas women buy or mainly influence about 80 per cent of household purchases, inversely 80 per cent of ad agency creative departments have historically tended to be male.

Mad Men are still a bit mad. Things have to change and they are. Happily, both men and women are now working together on that one. You can't move these days for articles and conferences about the importance of diversity in marketing and communications. Onwards and upwards.

IT'S A MAN MAN MAN MAN MAN MAN'S WORLD?

1   $12 trillion could be added to global GDP by 2025 by advancing women's equality.[4]

2   Representation by corporate role by gender and race in 2018 in the United States (the C-suite – direct reports to the CEO): 68 per cent white men, 9 per cent men of colour, 19 per cent white women, 4 per cent women of colour.[5]

3   For every 100 men promoted to manager, only 79 women are promoted to manager. Men end up holding 62 per cent of manager positions, while women hold only 38 per cent.[6]

4   In 279 companies, representing 13 million employees, women represent just 23 per cent of C-suite occupants and senior vice presidents, 29 per cent of the vice presidents, and 34 per cent of those at the senior manager and director levels.[7]

5   If women were to participate as equally as men in the workplace, that could drive $28 trillion in growth – the size of the economies of the United States and China put together. And, on average, there would be an 11 per cent increase in global GDP if every country achieved the fastest rate of progress towards gender equality in its workforce in its specific region.[8]

---

6   In 2017, the Korn Ferry Institute talked to 57 women CEOs – 41 who led *Fortune* 1,000 companies and 16 leading privately held companies – in order to determine traits and competencies of female corporate leaders. A common thread among women CEOs was risk-taking, resilience, agility and managing ambiguity. These leaders also embraced teamwork among their employees and they 'were more likely to leverage others to achieve desired results.'[9]

7   MIT sought to determine the make-up of the most effective leadership teams and found them to be best at reading people; and those were the teams with the most women.

8   Jack Zenger and Joseph Folkman wrote in the *Harvard Business Review* in 2012 about their research of more than 7,000 360-degree performance reviews that found women leaders outranked male leaders in nearly every one of 16 leadership competencies, including taking initiative and driving for results, competencies that are stereotypical male strengths.[10]

9   The Peterson Institute for International Economics completed a survey of 21,980 firms from 91 countries and found that having women at the C-suite level significantly increases net margins.[11]

10 Women are forecast to control over two-thirds of all consumer wealth in the United States over the next decade, according to Fleishman Hilliard.[12]

Money talks.

Whether we like it or not, money is a big route to power.

And studies prove that women who get into the top jobs tend to recruit and support more women and so the virtuous circle can happen. The cheering thing is that guys like the better balance at work. It's all good.

These are magic numbers indeed. And for everyone.

NOTES TO SELF

- Numbers are your friend. Make sure they're bosom pals.
- Money talks. Know how to talk about it (and make it, if you want).
- People talk as much through their behaviour as their mouths.
- Listen up.
- Inequality is never OK. Keep fighting the good fight (in a good way).

CHAPTER FIVE

Money talks

On learning the language called Finance

This chapter started its life attached to the previous one, but soon developed a life of its own.

That's because money and finance do tend to have their own special planet and language, even though their usage is universal.

You may already be a numbers whizz, have passed the exams and can find your way around financial statements like Warren Buffet. In which case, you can fast forward this chapter. Otherwise, read on for a short but hopefully to-the-point summary of accounting principles and terms.

I should just preface it with a health warning from my 'financial adviser'. They would like me to say, 'The specific reporting requirements and frequency vary depending on size of the company and whether the company is listed'. (I have focused on 'publicly listed' companies – ie the ones on stock exchanges – because you can easily find examples.) So now you know...

The basics

Companies need to do two main types of financial reporting to make sure they know:

a   what's going on with the business and its finances;
b   how to keep themselves out of jail by producing formal accounts that get filed in the UK Companies House, or other national equivalents.

Those two types of reporting are called (respectively and helpfully) *Management Accounts* and *Financial Accounts*. Management Accounts are created for a company's management and Financial Accounts are created for investors, creditors, and industry regulators.

- **Management Accounts** are for internal use only and give management a regular, month-by-month summary of what's happening with sales, costs, profits, cash, etc. They may give lots of detail by region, product, business unit and so on, evaluated against budgets and forecasts. You just need a decent spreadsheet or template for this (and/ or ideally a friendly book-keeper or finance department).
- **Financial Accounts** are much more concerned with informing those outside about the company's business performance and financial health – they're highly regulated. Unlike with Management Accounts, no future forecasting

is allowed in these legal statements – which is just as well, as growth plans can sometimes be management fantasy…

The following focuses mainly on the published, *financial* accounts because that's the stuff that boards are legally responsible for and therefore particularly interested in. They're also what the big accountancy firms like PwC, KPMG, EY and Deloitte are focused on auditing. And this is where the main jargon lives.

The formalities

Company annual reports and accounts

Company Annual Reports and Accounts (AR&A) are published on an annual basis, some months after that company's financial year-end (often 31 December, but it's at the discretion of the company). These Reports are good sources for understanding what the senior leadership of an organization say the company's doing and what is actually going on in the numbers. But over the years, the published Annual Report has frankly become more of a marketing document embedded with financial accounts. It's obviously lovely to see the Chairman's and CEO's photos and hear their statements about the organization having a strong purpose, great customer focus and well-being programmes for employees and local communities, or indeed that they are 'investing for future growth', 'finding efficiencies' and so on. But when wearing your 'temporary accountant' hat, you need to be the forensic detective.

Financial statements

There are three main financial statements to tell you what's going down in the sea of financial numbers. These are the *Income Statement*, the *Balance Sheet* and the *Cash Flow Statement*:

1 **The Income Statement (or Profit & Loss Account)** is a list of the *Sales Revenues* you are (hopefully) making, and the *Expenses* (ie overhead costs) you've incurred running the business (like staff salaries, travel, marketing, offices, IT and other plant and equipment, boring but necessary things like insurance, etc). The former will hopefully be more than the latter, which gives you some *Earnings* (ie profit) on which tax may be payable.

2 **The Balance Sheet** tells you how much you have or own (*Assets*) and how much you owe (*Liabilities*) as of the date of the Balance Sheet. Unlike the Income Statement, which is the accumulated revenues earned and costs incurred over the period stated, the balance sheet is a snapshot at a point in time. It's usually set out at the end of the company's financial year, but can also be looked at every one, three or six months (or on any one day if you really want to). If you take the *Liabilities* total away from the *Assets* total, whatever's left is the *Shareholders' Equity,* which is basically the net worth of the business. (NB: If you add the *Liabilities* total to the *Shareholders' Equity* total, that will add up to the *Assets total.* That's why it's called a Balance Sheet... because it balances.) Try not to confuse 'net worth' with a company's valuation or market capitalization (ie what investors believe it's worth paying for, or buying shares in it). See later glossary if confused.

TABLE 5.1 Example Group Income Statement

Group Income Statement		
COMPANY X – ILLUSTRATIVE ONLY	52 weeks ended	52 weeks ended
	31-Dec-19	31-Dec-18
	Total £m	Total £m
Total Revenue	91,819	84,310
Cost of goods/sales	(59,602)	(52,279)
Gross profit/(loss)	35,217	32,031
Expenses		
Research and development	(4,451)	(3,902)
Selling, general and administration	(4,140)	(3,815)
Depreciation and amortization	(1,057)	(968)
Total operating expenses	(9,648)	(8,685)
Operating profit	25,569	23,346
Finance income	885	1,160
Finance costs	(536)	(600)
Earnings/Profit(loss) before tax	25,918	23,906
Taxation	(3,682)	(3,941)
Profit/(loss) for the year	22,236	19,965
Earnings/(losses) per share		
Basic	5.04	4.22
Diluted	4.99	4.18

TABLE 5.2 Example Group Balance Sheet

Group Balance Sheet		
	31 December 2019	31 December 2018
COMPANY Y – ILLUSTRATIVE ONLY	£m	£m
Non-current assets		
Marketable securities	99,899	105,341
Property, plant and equipment	37,031	37,378
Other non-current assets	40,457	32,978
Total non-current assets	177,387	175,697
Current assets		
Cash and cash equivalents	39,771	48,844
Marketable securities	67,391	51,713
Accounts receivables, net	20,970	22,926
Inventories	4,097	4,106
Vendor non-trade receivables	18,976	22,878
Other current assets	12,026	12,352
Total current assets	163,231	162,819
Total Assets	340,618	338,516

(*continued*)

TABLE 5.2 (Continued)

Group Balance Sheet		
	31 December 2019	31 December 2018
COMPANY Y – ILLUSTRATIVE ONLY	£m	£m
Current liabilities		
Accounts payable	45,111	46,236
Other current liabilities	36,263	37,720
Deferred revenues	5,573	5,522
Commercial paper	4,990	5,980
Term debt	10,224	10,260
Total current liabilities	102,161	105,718
Non-current liabilities		
Term debt	93,078	91,807
Other non-current liabilities	55,848	50,503
Total non-current	148,926	142,310
Total liabilities	251,087	248,028
Net assets	89,531	90,488
Equity		
Share capital	45,972	45,174
Retained earnings	43,977	45,898
Accumulated and comprehensive income	(418)	(584)
Total shareholders equity	89,531	90,488

I know I was. In the early days of a business, or when it's going through a torrid time, the *Liabilities* may be more than the *Assets*, in which case, the *Shareholders' Equity* will be negative with brackets around the numbers as they are essentially bankrolling the company at that time.

3 **The Cash Flow Statement** tells you how much cash comes in and goes out of the business. That can be:

a. cash made from what you're actually selling;

TABLE 5.3 Example Group Cash Flow Statement

Group Cash Flow Statement	52 weeks 2019	52 weeks 2018
COMPANY Z – ILLUSTRATIVE ONLY	£m	£m
Operating Cashflow		
Net earnings	2,153	1,839
Plus depreciation and amortization	1,375	1,295
Less changes in Working Capital	(886)	175
Cash generated from operations	**2,642**	**3,309**
Interest paid	(306)	(328)
Corporation tax (paid)/ received	(370)	(176)
Net cash from operations	**1,966**	**2,805**

(continued)

TABLE 5.3 (continued)

Group Cash Flow Statement	52 weeks 2019	52 weeks 2018
COMPANY Z – ILLUSTRATIVE ONLY	£m	£m
Investing Cash Flow		
Investments in Property & Equipment	(1,143)	643
Cash from Investing	**(1,143)**	**643**
Financing Cash Flow		
Net cash generated from issuance (repayment) of debt or equity	(1,981)	(3,236)
Cash from Financing	**(1,981)**	**(3,236)**
Net increase (decrease) in cash	(1,158)	212
Opening cash balance	4,059	3,832
Effect of foreign exchange rate changes	15	15
Closing Cash Balance	**2,916**	**4,059**

    b. cash from investments (eg more permanent-type stuff like buildings and big equipment versus stuff you use every day, eg trading stock, inventory);

    c. borrowed cash from the bank/investors.

As I said earlier in the last chapter, cash is king or queen.

4 Looking at these three statements together, for any of the companies, here are a few things to look out for:

a. Consistent growth in *Earnings* (profit) over time; carrying reasonable levels of *Debt*; and not having to keep on spending huge levels on 'Research and Development' to stay alive (unless the business is in its early stages.) If you were Warren Buffet (who likes investing in companies for the long term), you'd be looking at these measures as signs of a long-term 'durable competitive advantage'.

b. It's good (to say the least) to look at *Gross* and *Operating Profit Margins:*

   i. You calculate *Gross Margin* by looking at the Profit & Loss Account/Income Statement. Divide *Gross Profit* by *Total Sales Revenues*, and that gives you a *Gross Profit Margin* %. The higher the gross margin, the more money left in the business to cover overhead expenses and profit. It is important to see consistent or improving margins, while declining margins demand an explanation.

   ii. The *Operating Margin*, ie the bottom line, is *Operating Profit* divided by *Revenues*. It is important to benchmark margins against your industry competitors. Retailers have smaller margins than fast-moving consumer goods (FMCG) or indeed software companies. Equally, 'high-growth' companies generally have much smaller operating margins than those with steady reasonable growth. Fast growers often say they are 'investing in growth'. If this is the case, you should understand what they are investing in!

c. You need to keep *Expenses* (costs) under control. Consistency over time is the key.

d. Recognize that the financial statements only cover the stuff that accountants feel they can measure and capture (reasonably) accurately. For example, the value of brands is not reflected in financial statements except when a company has acquired another business that owns one or more brands; when this happens it is captured in the category of 'intangible assets'.

Rather ludicrously, this means that with a company like Coca-Cola, even though the brand is what makes it an exceptionally valuable company (reflected in the share price and market capitalization), you wouldn't know explicitly it was the brand at work from the financial statements. You have to look at circumstantial evidence and the fact that having a strong brand generates demand and along with it long-term, consistently high margins, low debt, and less need for high levels of R&D investment. The epitome of Warren Buffet's 'Durable Competitive Advantage'. Accounting has its limits as well as its (necessary) uses.

Other terms you may want to know

Depreciation	Tangible/physical assets like buildings and equipment are deemed to 'wear out'. You need to recognize the reducing value of those assets on the balance sheet. That's called *Depreciation.*
Amortization	The same 'wearing out' principle, but applied to Intangible Assets like patents, brand names, customer lists, software etc. However, ideally these don't reduce in value – you just spread the cost over time and reflect that in the balance sheet.

(*continued*)

EBIT (Earnings Before Interest and Taxes) *and* EBITDA (EBIT plus Depreciation and Amortization)	The former is easy – EBIT is your total income from doing business, but before you have deducted the necessary tax and deducted/ added any interest payments. (Warren Buffet doesn't like the 'DA' in EBITDA because you might have to spend lots on equipment and other assets to stay in business... and so it's not a true reflection of underlying value.)
Accounts Receivable *and* Accounts Payable	AR is money owed to the company for goods or services sold, but that haven't been paid for yet. AP is money owed by the company to its suppliers/creditors etc.
Goodwill	The value of any asset over and above the value that is shown on the 'books' (ie Accounts). This will only be shown or realized on the balance sheet if the acquiring company buys an asset for more than it seems to be worth from the 'book' value (that's why Accounting can be dumb sometimes).
Accrued Expenses	This is an expense (cost) that has been incurred, and you know you will have to pay it eventually, but has not yet been formally recorded in the Accounts (as opposed to Accounts Payable, where someone has issued an invoice and it's just in the queue to be paid).
Equity/Equity Capital/ Shareholders' Equity	This is the net worth (ie the difference between the assets and liabilities) of the business. The financial value that is 'owned' by shareholders (whoever they may be) and is different from the company's market valuation.

(continued)

Retained Earnings	All the accumulated Earnings (net profits) of a business over time that have not been paid out as dividends (you clearly want to see long-term growth in these). Shown in the Shareholders' Equity Section of the balance sheet – the same as 'Issued Share Capital'.
Dividend	The payment by a company to its shareholders, usually as a distribution of (some of) the profits. It's obviously nice to do this regularly and consistently once a business has matured.
Working Capital	Basically, the money available to a company for day-to-day operations – essentially, the money you have to work with. In financial speak, it's the difference between current Assets and current Liabilities.
Return on Equity (ROE) or Return on Capital (ROC)	ROE is a company's net income, divided by the Shareholders' Equity. The higher the better, as you can imagine. All these measures are calculated slightly differently, but all reflect the profitability of a company based on the money it had to work with. ROC just includes the value of debts owed.
Fiscal	Usually refers to government/public finance, but companies essentially have to report their financials according to national government's fiscal (ie tax) years.
Leverage	The amount of debt the company has in relation to the shareholders' equity. A company that is 'highly leveraged' basically means that it is carrying a lot of debt (which can obviously be quite risky, particularly if it has to pay high interest on that debt).

(*continued*)

Coupon	The annual interest rate paid on a Bond (which is a unit of corporate debt issued by companies, and used as tradeable assets, if you wanted to know the technical bit). Coupon rate is usually expressed as a percentage.
Audit/Internal Audit	An Audit is the examination of a company's Accounting records, as well as the physical inspection of its assets. Qualified chartered accountants can express an opinion on the fairness of a company's financial statements. Internal Audits evaluate a company's internal controls, including its corporate governance and accounting processes. They ensure compliance with law and regulations, and generally help with accuracy in financial reporting. (They also keep you out of jail, ideally. Internal Audit people are your friends.)
Shareholders/ Investors	These are usually referred to interchangeably, but strictly, the term investor is more broadly used as a person/institution who invests money in order to make a profit while shareholder refers to the ownership of shares. You need to be nice to both.
Analysts (Buy-side and Sell-side)	Analysts usually cover publicly traded companies. It's easy to bunch 'analysts' together – these are obviously the people who do analyses and make recommendations on which companies to invest in. However, there's a big difference in the job, and who employs each. *A buy-side analyst* usually works for institutional investors such as hedge funds, pension funds, or mutual funds. They do research and make recommendations to the money managers of the fund that employs them. They're very concerned about 'being right'

(*continued*)

because their job depends on good forensic advice (and not making mistakes). In contrast, *sell-side analysts* work for a brokerage or firm that manages individual accounts and makes recommendations to the clients of the firm. You'll hear stuff like 'strong buy,' 'outperform,' 'neutral,' or 'sell' from these people. The job of a sell-side analyst is to convince institutional accounts to direct their trading through the trading desk of the analyst's firm – the job is very much about marketing. And, of course, they're not lynched if wrong (like the poor buy-side peeps).

Market Capitalization/ Market Cap (and vs Shareholder Equity): Market Cap	Is the total value of all outstanding shares of a company. It's calculated by multiplying the current share price by the number of outstanding shares. Not surprisingly, *Market Cap* is nearly always greater than *Equity* value. Analysts tend to use *Market Cap* to describe a company's size, although it can be volatile because it's dependent on share price. Share price is dependent on demand for the shares and expectations of future revenues and profits.

In contrast, *Shareholders' Equity* doesn't fluctuate day to day – it's a simple statement of a company's *Assets* minus its *Liabilities* and represents the accounting value of one's stake in an investment. The market often refers to total shareholder value; the combination of capital gain (increase in share price minus purchase price) and dividends. So hopefully, owning stock in a company over time will yield *capital gains* for the shareholder and potentially dividends. A shareholder may also get the right to vote in board of directors' elections (so if there enough of them, they can kick people out if they're doing a crap job).

(*continued*)

Earnings Per Share (EPS)	A commonly used measure of corporate performance – EPS is a company's profit divided by its number of common outstanding shares (eg if a company earning £2 million in one year had 2 million common shares of stock outstanding, its EPS would be £1 per share). So, it breaks down a firm's profits on a per share basis. It's important to investors because the higher the earnings per share of a company, the better its profitability.
Total Shareholder Return (TSR)	Another popular indicator of company performance. It measures the total return generated by a stock to an investor, and factors in capital gains and dividends too.

Phew.

Money never sleeps

Do seek out some decent courses and accountant friends for a lot more. And remember that you also need to make sure you have access to some good legal advice if you're going to run a business. Whilst it might not get you an 'out of jail free' card, it can be useful for those moments of doubt.

NOTES TO SELF

- You're not stupid (and you're so not alone) if it takes you a while to get this stuff.

- Accountant-speak can just be 'creative' in a different way. It's about learning the language.

- When in doubt, cash is the thing that never lies. If nothing else, look at the cash flow statement. You know that bit makes sense.

CHAPTER SIX

Why you don't have to fake it to make it

On how to be your (best) self... most of the time

There was a television series in the UK called *Faking It*, which began in 2000. It was about personal transformation, and it was riveting, scary and heart-warming all at the same time. It featured a range of 'ordinary' people who were trained to pretend they were something they weren't and at the end of four weeks, a panel of expert judges tried to identify the faker from a group of three. Many of them managed to fool the judges.

A cellist 'trained' to be a club DJ, with all the technical know-how and associated clothes, personal presentation and attitude. A humble burger-van owner became a ranting

Gordon Ramsay-type chef. A straight-laced naval officer transformed into a convincing drag queen and a young 'working class' woman was taught how to behave in 'high society' (whatever that means today). In fact, the series idea was inspired by *Pygmalion*, where, of course, the flower girl Eliza Doolittle is schooled (by a grumpy professor) to appear like an aristocrat.

The thing to note about this series was that:

- the participants had intense and expert coaching on their 'new' role over a concentrated period;
- they often cried a lot, broke down, said they couldn't do it, and generally got anxious and tense throughout the show;
- we didn't really see what happened to them after the broadcast.

Making the most of the real you

Having said all this, it served to demonstrate the rather obvious lesson that we all have potential to learn, grow, change, make more of ourselves than our lives allow. I totally support that, but of course, if you have just turned in an 80-hour week and you're quite busy trying to keep the show on the road as it is, you have limited time and energy to learn Serbo-Croat or train to become a NASA astronaut as a hobby.

As a working mother, earlier in my career it was all I could do to stay awake and pretend I was paying attention. I did watch a fair amount of rubbish television late at night, but that was my way (and we all have our own ways) of switching off. I have mixed emotions when I hear of people who have hugely demanding jobs, several children to ferry around for tennis, dancing and violin lessons, friends' parties and still manage to do an MBA in their 'spare' time: presumably between the hours of 3 and 6 am in the morning.

Actually, this is impressive and good for them, but I'm going to focus on slightly more ordinary mortals who would still like to do as well as they can. But who also need to sleep and have downtime occasionally.

You may well have heard the slightly annoying term 'fake it till you make it'. Or, indeed, the equally preachy 'act as if'. I'm going to make one of the few uses of my classical education here by telling you that this concept reflects Aristotle's philosophy that people 'acquire' a particular quality by constantly acting a certain way.

Clearly, there is a lot of science and research that goes into treatments like Cognitive Behavioural Therapy (CBT), and the practice of Neuro-Linguistic Programming (NLP). All ways of helping you reframe your current beliefs, attitudes and behaviours and develop some different and more positive habits.

People like the American self-help guru Tony Robbins (and the British version, Paul McKenna) have made fortunes through stadium tours, books and TV shows whilst they've awoken our inner giants and helped us to think ourselves Thin/Happy/Rich/Confident and able to Sleep (my personal favourite one of Paul's). Mr McKenna can also even *Change Your Life in 7 Days* if you're short of time.

The peculiar power of self-development

I must confess, I'm a bit of personal development junkie and a few of my activities have included lying on a sofa gushing out my inner feelings to a psychotherapist, writing an angry-yet-therapeutic letter to my dead father, scream-ing myself hoarse on a 'creativity' course, and painting a picture of my 'ideal future' on a career development course that sort of acted like a reverse work portrait of Dorian Gray in my attic. I've also walked over hot coals in a car park at the ExCeL Centre in London at a Tony Robbins seminar. He is a very persuasive man.

I've also read most of the famous self-help and discovery books including *The Road Less Travelled*, *Feel the Fear* (I didn't do it anyway) and *The Celestine Prophecy* amongst many profound others.[1]

I have even worked with the spiritual guru-to-the-stars Deepak Chopra, and tried to follow his *Seven Spiritual Laws of Success*, even though I secretly much preferred the sublime four-handed Ayurvedic Shirodhara/Panchakarma massage and warm oil-dripping treatment on my third eye at his retreat in La Jolla, California. I even managed to present this as a necessary 'brand familiarization and induction' process to my company. My creative director at the time went in to have the treatment before me, and he was so blissed out when he came out that he could hardly speak. On a more practical level, I may have achieved around two of the *Seven Habits of Highly Effective People*.

You may think that the non-exhaustive list above sounds a lot, but as a general point, it really can be a good idea to do some self-development work at various times in your life and career. Apart from the benefit of learning new tools and techniques for changing behaviour and mindsets both personally and professionally, it's just useful to spend some time on yourself, perhaps by yourself or with very different groups of people. I've usually got a lot out of it.

Here are my observations:

1 It's worth getting difficult personal stuff under more positive control before you visit it too much on those around you. I found out quite a lot about psychotherapy early on. The upside is that you can unpack all your formative experiences, good, bad and ugly, including those that you had completely forgotten about. Once you can see them, you can try and make a more conscious choice about whether and how you're going to let them drive you. It obviously doesn't work for everyone, but it really helped me. For some, psychotherapy can become a bit circular – sooner or later, you need to get into a more practical 'what do I do about all this/how do I change those unhelpful habits' mode.

2 If you feel things are basically alright but feel the need to do some more sorting-type stuff, there is also a range of events like Landmark Forum and all its derivatives.[2] Some people swear by these and come out feeling totally cleansed and purposeful. Others loathe and detest them. They all tend to have a variant on the 'acknowledge that you could be more in life, visualize a new future and commit to doing something to get there' sequence. I didn't particularly need any more help in being self-critical, and my poor mother was rather nonplussed that I was calling her late at night asking for forgiveness, as the courses sometimes require you to do. It can all

feel a bit weird and 'culty'. But it's another way to open yourself to the idea of (real versus fake) change. The health warning is that, from these sessions, people can decide to up and leave their partners, jobs and so on. You have been warned.

3 Attending sessions with gurus can be both entertaining and genuinely valuable experiences. For example, Tony Robbins is brilliant, but quite scary. He is, literally, a physical giant, as well as offering to help get your own 'inner giant' to wake up, smell the coffee and get Unlimited Power. Oprah, Bill Clinton, Leonardo DiCaprio and numerous business leaders have apparently used his services. If you attend one of his courses (which I did out of a combination of curiosity and a special offer), he walks around the huge stadium-size audience and towers over people like an over-sized rock god, shaking hands, pulling willing people out of the audience. People at his sessions get to believe he can make an immediate difference to negative feelings by making them carry themselves differently and think themselves into a different mindset. It's all a bit surreal, with pumping rock music accompanying his stage shows all the way through, and constant audience applause. Seeing him live overpowered any power I was looking for. It awoke my Britishness (versus 'Giant') Within. Having said all that, there are some useful facts, figures and examples about role-modelling and positive visualization in his books which I found really helpful. And perhaps surprisingly, he can also be quite funny, which is just as well when you're about to run over hot coals in your bare feet and need a sense of humour about the prospect of going to hospital with blistered soles (and no, this doesn't really happen).

You pays your (significant, in his case) money and you takes your chance. Apparently, he has a net worth of around \$500 million,[3] so clearly enough people are indeed 'taking' it.

MY THREE SUPERSIZE TAKEAWAYS FROM TONY ROBBINS' WORK

- If you change your physiology (posture), you can completely change your energy and mindset. If that sounds a bit like the old-fashioned 'head up, chest out, heart up', well, that's modern packaging for you.

- If there's someone you particularly admire, study what they do that works and try and model or copy them a bit. That's potentially your short cut to success (but don't be too weird about it).

- People want to move towards pleasure and move away from pain. So, whatever you would like to do (or want anyone else to do), it's sensible to frame your request in that way – in other words, what's in it for you and/or them that the change in behaviour will deliver. This apparently works particularly well for addictive behaviour...

---

4 Worth a bit less (although still apparently around £65 million,[4] so not struggling to get by), a bit less scary and definitely not as tall, is Paul McKenna. He 'did a gig' for my company some years ago, when he was just changing people's lives in seven days, rather than diversifying and expertly segmenting his business into his promises of

making us all Thin/Rich/Happy/whatever. Actually, he was super-entertaining in person, hypnotized a couple of people, and did a rather interesting exercise of helping everyone in the (very packed) room get rid of bad memories and experiences. In fact, the session was standing room only – much more so than any other 'serious' business speaker we'd had. Self-improvement stuff was clearly more popular than people would care to admit.

5 I found it particularly worthwhile getting some training on positive visualization techniques. This might be things like drawing or painting a 'future' picture of your ideal life or assembling images of what you'd like your future life to have in it. Or, it could be learning how to 'run a videotape' in your head about how you'd ideally like to do a presentation (more on this in the 'Voices Off' chapter), or perhaps doing a bit of breathing and 'white light' bathing/visualization when you think you might otherwise scream, cry or murder someone. Honestly, it can come in handy.

But, inevitably, any work on yourself to get on and succeed has got to be based on a premise of effort and some level of reality and authenticity. You might want to visualize yourself as an Olympic athlete, but unless you have the physical attributes and are prepared to dedicate your life to training, it's probably not going to happen.

Are you a hockey player or a triathlon champion?

I listened to a panel of Team GB Olympic medal winners after the 2016 Rio Games talk about what helped them succeed. If you are British, you might remember the excitement and thrill of the Women's Hockey team winning a gold medal against the Netherlands after a penalty shoot-out, where the goal keeper Maddie Hinch was a total heroine. The women's team talked about how important their team psychologist had been, how much work they had all done, individually and together, about their anxieties, issues, motivations, shared vision for the future, how they worked on their victory visualization and mindsets. Whilst not without considerable emotional challenge and investment, they all felt the psychological help and process had worked brilliantly for them.

The interviewer then turned to the Brownlee brothers, Alistair and Jonny, who had won the gold and silver medals respectively for the Triathlon.

They were asked whether they had made similar use of a psychologist in their training and preparation. They were dignified enough to control any sniggers. Eventually, Alistair said something along the lines of, 'No, my main psychology was, you've worked incredibly hard doing all that training, so just don't f*** it up.'

I'm married to a Yorkshireman. I get it.

There we have it. Only you will know whether you're a Hockey or a Triathlon. The thing that they shared, though, is desire to succeed, a work, work, work ethic and gut-busting effort all round, over a sustained period. You can't fake the latter two.

Stretching the truth

Clearly, it's difficult to completely change the reality of who you are, what you're good at, and your natural comfort zones. However, you can stretch yourself in a whole range of ways to give that 'reality' more possibilities. And to be more honest about both. So, not to have to 'fake' it, with all the stresses and strains that can bring.

There have been various occasions when I recognized myself 'faking it'. I remember interviewing candidates towards the end of my time at Saatchi & Saatchi, after the forced departure of the founders – a long and sad story. My heart had gone out of the business, and my head was heading elsewhere, but I still found myself having to give the spiel on why this was a great place. I began to hate listening to myself; it's a strange but distinctive feeling when your voice doesn't sound like you, and your inner voice is insisting that you're sounding like a fake. That's when you know it's time to do something else.

When I was considering an offer to leave my strategy director job, and become CEO at another company, I remember a business friend telling me that, honestly, she thought I'd hate being CEO. It would mean stopping doing much practitioner stuff , which I enjoyed and was good at, and instead having to deal with constant client complaints, financials, management systems, employee moans and groans. In some ways, she was right, of course, although she did have a slight ulterior motive.

She and I had been planning to start a business together, and we had spent several months meeting in confidence to create what it would look like. It was an exciting time, and she was brilliantly talented and generally terrific. The challenge was, we were not exactly complementary in a professional sense, and when it came to some critical decision points, we were honest with each other about recognizing that we both enjoyed doing similar things; at that time, neither of us were as experienced or interested in the commercial/operational side of the business as would have been ideal. So we agreed that she would introduce some other people into the mix.

To cut a very long and emotionally challenging story short, having tried to make the business idea work with this wider group of people, it didn't really work for me any longer. In the end, the only reason for doing the new business would have been not to let this woman down, rather than because I really wanted to do it. Not a great long-term proposition, and a recipe for later resentment on both sides.

So, after a lot of agonizing, I pulled out. It was a horrible decision.

Instead, I accepted the CEO role that she said I would hate. And honestly, most of the time I did. This may well have been divine revenge, and I think I can safely say that I fantasized about resigning every day for at least six months.

On top of the basic CEO job and learning about how to be directly in day-to-day charge of the ship, and in a new type of business, I also had to work with a pretty complex management set-up. I found myself having to deal with the after effects of a merger that I would not have decided to do myself, with the fallout of a PR disaster that I had no part in creating, and with warring factions of people who didn't want to be together. All owned by a demanding US publicly quoted group holding company, who wanted to see reliable quarterly earnings, and hear no excuses.

The perils of bending yourself (and snapping)

I became a nervous (and sleepless) wreck, but was determined to disguise it, and play the role of competent, determined and (hopefully positive) ass-kicking CEO.

At that time, I developed a serious friendship with a Mr Bach and we have been very close ever since. That's actually Bach's Rescue Remedy. It's a flower-based natural remedy that's supposed to have a calming influence (the label says 'Comfort & Reassure'). And, strangely enough, I did find that it helped in some weird and wonderful way.

In fact, it wasn't so weird when I looked more closely at the ingredients. In addition to the lovely flower extracts like Rock Rose, Impatiens, Clematis, Star of Bethlehem and Cherry Plum (aaaah, nice...), there was... 27 per cent alcohol content. That might have possibly explained its 'efficacy', and at some later point when I found myself on a flight out of New York and the cabin crew appeared at speed through the cabin just after take-off carrying fire extinguishers, I was so grateful to those 'flowers'. I necked most of the bottle while my pounding heart was about to burst through my chest.

I still swear by Rescue Remedy today, and use it (along with deep yogic breathing, of course) before a lot of otherwise potentially angst-making situations, particularly big meetings, speeches and flying.

There are many different ways and means of keeping yourself calm and focused, and I find it useful to have a 'ritual'. For example, some tennis players bounce balls in a particular sequence. Some people use squeeze balls, some do fixed exercises. Find your own thing.

Tip top...

Back to the day job, I was trying to look, sound and play the part of an on-top-of-it CEO. Doing a tough merger, learning the new business, getting on top of the finances and operations, worrying about the state of the bathrooms as well as the vision thing, and trying to see the children and my husband as much as I could. And just for good measure, I thought I should get a book out. It was nearing the Millennium, and I thought that it was a good time to look back and forward at the future of brands and branding. Frankly, I needed my head examining. But that was the annoying and needy drive talking. As it happened, the *Future of Brands* book that emerged was successful and it was great to have done it.[5]

All in all, a bit full-on and stressful. And yet something in the job eventually clicked with me. Earlier in the recruitment phase for my CEO role, the head-hunter was much more convinced about my ability to do the job than I was. Initially, I was uncertain and not particularly interested.

But I did grow into it after a fashion. And lo, I was able to put into practice lots of the things I felt strongly about:

- lots of participation and collaboration;
- evenly balanced numbers of men and women on the management team;
- a supportive workplace culture that had things like personal bursaries, yoga and even choirs.

And for a few years, the business grew and performed well. And very few people that we didn't want to lose, left. I found I could just about live with the demands of the role, relentless or not.

... Rock bottom

And then, in fairly quick succession, a couple of mortal blows for the business. First, the dotcom expansion of the nineties and noughties turned into the dot bomb explosion, where financial markets lost confidence. And, later that year, much worse, when two planes flew into the Twin Towers in New York on 9/11. One of those events when you can remember so vividly where you were.

Apart from the appalling and horrifying event itself for humanity, the business consequences of 9/11, on top of the dotcom market collapse, were dire for people and their jobs in certain sectors. Including ours. Suddenly, we had to switch from a so-called 'war for talent' (which we had been winning) to a war to reduce costs in the shortest possible time to help the business survive (which was impossible for anyone to feel was 'winning').

Even now, I can remember that the Nelly Furtado track *I'm Like a Bird* was playing as I walked around our office feeling shell-shocked by the prospect of having to make more than 25 per cent of our people redundant. Many of those people I had recruited, trained, developed and loved.

Whilst I had always found the role of CEO to be an interesting blend of therapist and driver, now came the additional (unwelcome) role of executioner. That was truly a 'faking it' job for me at the time, and I struggled to keep it up with my US owners who were understandably wanting to see costs disappearing, along with a lot of people.

The decisive moment came when I was driving home late one night and got a call from a global group director. In response to my protest that we were reducing costs at a responsible rate bearing in mind trying to mitigate the human cost and European employment legislation – sometimes an infuriating thing for US companies to accept – I heard the following rant: 'Rita, for the foreseeable future, this business is about the ruthless pursuit of profit'.

There was silence while I worked out what to say, that didn't have a swear word in it.

Great escape?

I tell you this story in a bit more detail than I originally intended for a couple of reasons:

- First, to notice when a role goes over the edge from a stretch zone to a no-go (ie need for totally fake) zone.
- Second, that it's important to understand yourself and what you can/can't/will/ won't do. But preferably, rationally and coolly.

Yes, it is quite a good idea to make sure you think things through properly before any storming out. No matter how many times you might fantasize about the 'well, if that's the way you feel, then you can just get lost' and slam the door on the way out etc, it's usually not a good idea. Unless you have a rock-solid financial cushion and bulletproof reputation already, you need to plan your next move before throwing it all in.

I resigned twice over the next six weeks, thinking that I'd rather start a business myself and feel more in control than have to bend myself out of shape to a big and muscular corporate owner. I even had a plan for what that business might be. But you know, a pragmatic outcome emerged when they eventually said that they didn't want to lose me, that perhaps I might consider becoming chairman instead of CEO, and doing more of the things I liked rather than being the main person with the axe. Being a sucker for feeling wanted, and also a sucker for liking a safe salary that paid for the mortgage and my part of our family life, I agreed. It was an easy decision, perhaps too easy, but actually, the chair role really suited me and set off a load of opportunities that really worked out. Another potential benefit of taking a deep breath and not being too hasty. On this occasion, I confess I decided to fake some confidence when I didn't feel it.

Of course, in the end, fully faking it is all very well for four weeks of a TV show, but trying to live a faked life long term is guaranteed to make you miserable and even ill. But you can bring who you are to a whole lot of different and interesting things that you might not have believed possible.

Gritting teeth

Moral of the story?

Sometimes, it's good to put yourself into uncomfortable roles because, whether it makes you feel fulfilled every day or not, you learn a lot, grow a lot, and understand what you're able and willing to do. All those clichés apply. It can also be a stepping stone to something else.

My husband has always joked that I was a slightly rubbish junior project manager, but that I got better and better in more senior roles. We agreed that this was probably because I genuinely loved working with people, understanding them and seeing how I could help them develop. He said he felt the opposite about himself, in case you think he was being undermining. But the practical lesson is, not every job might be your heart's desire. It might be a conveyor belt.

Years later, when I was having one of my regular bouts of coaching, I did an exercise called 'Career Anchors'.[6] It's a relatively simple test that prioritizes a person's preference for eight themes, and it brought home to me in simple terms why I had disliked being CEO so much. It tells you what you should ideally spend most of your working life doing if you're to be happy and authentic. For example, some people need to have creativity at the heart of what they do, some people need to be an expert practitioner. And some people need so badly to run things that they can put up with all sorts of shit.

I wasn't one of those people. But... I did manage to end up running the type of business where I could do both practitioner stuff as well as putting up a vaguely decent show of trying to look as though I was in charge. Not an ideal balance, but doable, and in a way that bore a passing resemblance to the 'me' inside. Even with gritted teeth.

JUST LISTEN TO YOURSELF

The 'real me' loved strategy, coaching, mentoring and evangelism about good business. The 'fake me' CEO pretended to kick ass.

Becoming Chair enabled me to know how to help others kick asses nicely. One test I found helpful was to listen to your own voice when you are talking to people about stuff. You can honestly hear the phoney tone in yourself when you're putting on an act. Try it. Even if you have to say and do tough stuff when you don't feel very tough, find a way to talk about it in your authentic voice (eg 'I know we have to make some people redundant to reflect the reduction in business, but it's a truly horrible thing for the people involved as well as for the reputation of the business. So we are going to do it as generously and openly as we can.')

I would obviously hate you to take from all this that you have to make yourself miserable for your whole working life to serve at the altar of 'more women in charge please'. But it is possible to shape a leading role in a way that suits you better.

To be as influential as you'd like to be (as the world might need you to be) is more possible than you think. Do it your own way. And you can even try on different versions of yourself along the way. There's a great saying that, 'It's better to be yourself, because you'll never be as good at trying to be someone else.' Very true. But we're not all fixed beings from birth, and we can and do grow and adapt. Hopefully, for the better.

Of course, you can't be Dr Jekyll and Ms Hyde. I am working on the assumption that you are a decent person, wanting things to be as good as they can be in the world. In the end, of course, in this open, transparent, digital world, the truth will out, so it's best to try and make the reality as good as it can be.

Friends like this...

I'll just end this chapter with a real-life illustration about the ups and downs of short-term fakery. It doesn't need too much introduction, except to tell you that, soon after I became CEO, *The Daily Telegraph* ran a feature on how senior women coped with stress. They said they wanted to run a profile, and came in to interview me and take a picture. Apart from wanting to get a full chemical peel, sleep therapy and all-over liposuction when I saw the photo (and also get my money back from 'House of Colour', who recommended the make-up), I think I even managed to convince myself of some of what I was saying. My husband, who actually had to live with me, had a slightly different perspective. He saw the article, developed one of those mysterious rueful smiles, and wrote his own version, especially for me. I dug it out again after all these years and thought I'd share the side-by-side comparison.

First, the *Daily Telegraph* version, having interviewed me...

IS THE PRESSURE GETTING TO YOU? People take more time off as a result of stress than they do for colds, reports Christine Doyle

By Christine Doyle

Source: Martin Pope/Telegraph Media Group Limited

12:00AM GMT 31 Oct 2000

[...]

'Energised by a challenge'

Outgoing and tireless, Rita Clifton is chief executive of Interbrand, a marketing company that advises on brand names (Prozac, a medical antidote to stress, is one example). Pressure and challenge energize her – a good thing since she has a staff of 270, a mixture of financial and creative high-fliers. Only rarely does she feel overwhelmed. 'There are days when I feel absolutely "full up" by the time I get home and cannot imagine doing another thing. But it does not last long. I love the stress of the job – it is almost addictive.'

Clifton, 42, takes pains, however, to acknowledge that she is privileged: 'I do not have to face looking after a child with very little money.' Her stable childhood and present happy family life – she has two daughters – have all helped to keep her life in balance. Her second husband, whom she met when working at Saatchi & Saatchi, understands her work. 'I have also had very good nannies.'

She describes herself as a 'do it now' person. 'Getting things out of the way prevents stress. If someone calls to make an appointment to see me about their career, my inclination is to ask them to come and talk there and then.'

Remembering things is, she admits, becoming much more difficult. 'So I carry a little Dictaphone tape to capture any new thought.' She was not particularly organized as a child, she recalls: 'I learned that later.' But, like her mother, she has always had 'a positive take on life'.

If she is feeling overwhelmed, she might close her eyes and take deep breaths. Bach's flower therapy, Rescue Remedy, helps her through airport delays. A good night's sleep is a must, and exercise, especially a brisk walk, is 'fantastically effective if I'm worried about something'. Her indulgences are shopping at Harvey Nichols and a personal trainer.

And now my husband's version, having lived with me...

'Shattered by a challenge'

Rita Clifton is the outgoing Chief Executive of Interbrand, a marketing company that advises on brand names (Prozac, a medical antidote to stress, is one example). 'I'd love to say that pressure and challenge energize me,' says Clifton, 'but the reality is the reverse' – something of a problem given that she has a staff of 270, a mixture of financial and creative high-fliers. There's rarely a day, she says, when she doesn't feel overwhelmed. 'There are the occasional moments when I feel positive and energetic, but it doesn't last long. Even then I'm only good for three slices of toast and marmite and a slump on the sofa at the end of the day. I'd like to jack the whole thing in, but the status and prestige that comes with the position is addictive.'

Clifton, a tired-looking 42, acknowledges that she feels unhappy and unfulfilled much of the time. Her unstable childhood and unsatisfying present family life – she has two daughters whom she hardly sees – also contribute to her deep malaise. Her current husband has little sympathy for her predicament. Nevertheless, she is at pains to point out that she is privileged: 'At least I don't have to face looking after my children all of the time, for little emotional reward and absolutely no money.'

She describes herself as a 'sweep it under the carpet till the lump becomes a mountain' type person. 'Getting things out of the way is not my strong point' she insists. 'If someone calls to make an appointment to see me about their career my inclination is to put them off for as long as possible in the hope they'll end up taking their whinges and whines elsewhere.'

Remembering things is, she admits, becoming more difficult. 'I'm convinced I've got early Alzheimer's. My mother's barking mad and I guess it's only a matter of time before I go the same way.' She carries, she says, a little Dictaphone to capture any new thoughts she has.

'Without it, I'd forget half the chores I need to get my husband to do each day.'

She wasn't particularly organized as a child, and that has remained unchanged in later life. 'I've learned to depend on other people to organize my life and to get things done.'

If she is feeling overwhelmed she finds solace in crisps and several glasses of champagne. 'I find that alcohol and fatty foods are fantastically effective if I'm worried about something', she says. This, and her aversion to any form of exercise, lead to constant sleepless nights.

'The only time I'm really happy is when I'm on a binge at Harvey Nichols. I must get round to fixing myself up with a personal shopper', she concludes.

Oh, how I laughed. We're all human.

NOTES TO SELF

- Get some help… whether from professional/personal/self-development specialists and more alternative stuff or mentors and empathetic friends. Learning comes in strange and wonderful ways (and you can always edit out the weird shit).

- Think stretch rather than fake. Not every job's a joy, but make sure it's for a reason.

- Know thyself… eventually. You can be all kinds of leader if you want to be.

CHAPTER SEVEN

Voices off

On how anyone can learn to be a good communicator. Honestly

You just have to watch some of the stiff, nervous interviews and speeches of people in public life when under
fire to understand that it's a good idea to get confident with
public speaking. And by that, I don't mean declamation, or
being able to read aloud.

I'm not suggesting that everyone needs to be an orator
like Martin Luther King, John Kennedy, or even that
wonderfully theatrical preacher who spoke at Prince Harry
and Meghan Markle's wedding. Equally, you just have to
watch former British Prime Minister Theresa May speaking
for a few minutes to feel both nervous for her, irrespective

of your politics, and irritated at the object lesson in bland generalization.

Barack Obama is obviously sublime (particularly at making autocue look sincere). Theresa May's predecessor, David Cameron, seemingly won the leadership of his political party by being able to make a decent speech without notes. French President Emmanuel Macron similarly wowed people to vote for him because he gave great speeches. However, in politics, Tony Blair takes the award for being able to find the right words and tone whenever needed: for example, in the aftermath of Princess Diana's tragic death in 1997, he coined the immortal phrase 'People's Princess'. Even if you are still angry with Blair about the Gulf War, the fact that he was so persuasive and compelling boosted his support at the time. In addition to the small matter of winning three general elections, of course.

As a quick 'voices off' voice off, Tony Blair was also much derided when he became 'mockney' when talking to 'the people'. This, some reasoned, was an example of his lack of authenticity – after all, he was a posh boy from a superior private school in Edinburgh. Why go so chummy-y?

I have a slightly different perspective on this, and because of an unashamedly vested interest. You see, I used to conduct market research focus groups as part of one of my roles. This is where groups of around eight people from your 'target audience' sit around in someone's living room discussing anything from washing powder to bank accounts and political parties.

I was facilitating one in the east end of London, and at the end of the session, I went back behind the two-way mirror where some of my colleagues had been observing the session to get a first-hand view of their consumers. I should emphasize that this observation was always done with consent – no sinister hidden persuading going on. I found them giggling like crazy, and when I asked them what was so funny about questioning unfortunate people about dandruff, they said, 'It wasn't that, it was that your accent got stranger and stranger as the group went on!'

I must confess, I was slightly and pathetically hurt. I hadn't really been aware of doing it, and I certainly hadn't been 'putting on an accent'. It was just that I seemed to have unconsciously absorbed the atmosphere and tone of voice in the room, and it felt more comfortable for doing that.

I discovered later that this is exactly the sort of thing you are taught in Neuro-Linguistic Programming (NLP) ie to mirror people's body language and voice cadence. People are paid good money for teaching that stuff – and I was doing it as part of normal life! Frankly, I didn't have a clue where my supposed 'posh' normal accent came from either, but my mixed childhood and teenage experiences gave me something of a library to draw on. I'm not sure where Tony Blair's accent bank is from, but I did have sympathy for his sponge-like qualities.

Nothing wrong with showing empathy and connection, and never more important than when you're trying to get your points across to a room full of people.

LESSONS FROM PERICLES

In ancient Greece, the birthplace of modern democracy, they devised a system of direct democracy and voting (a 'one man, one vote' system – sadly, at that time it really did only mean 'man' in the literal sense – and using stones as voting slips). The generals would address the assembled hordes and try and get their votes on actions like whether they should wage war on other city states and aggressors. The ancient historical commentator Thucydides said that, 'It was in theory a democracy, but in practice, the power was all in the hands of its greatest citizen.' That citizen was Pericles, and that power was because he was a great orator who could stir and persuade the crowd to his will.

That's original populism for you. Very powerful and, of course, potentially very dangerous. The devil can have all the best tunes. And the digital world now enables demagoguery on a grand scale.

Hopefully, if you are or can become a great orator, you'll use that power for good. No pressure.

Show up as a human.

Being able to talk like a human being (that knows what they're talking about) is a core skill not just for leaders, but for anyone who wants to be as effective and influential as they can.

A sad and serious example sticks in my mind. In 2006, two children lost their lives in Corfu, Greece when a faulty boiler poisoned them. As a human being, it was awful. As a parent, it was an impossible watch. The Swiss CEO of the company, Peter Fankhauser, was put up in front of a press conference to explain. Outside the conference, the children's family were all too human in their grief. In contrast, the CEO read a stilted prepared speech from a press release, from an autocue, against a cold blue corporate background. You could almost hear the lawyers in his ear, telling him to stick to the script. A real human was needed to speak here, and that human failed to show up. To his later credit, he confessed that he had wanted to speak on a personal level, and apologized personally and profusely in person to the family. He was human after all.

On a lighter note, trying too hard to be seen to talk like a human when deep down you think that your product is rubbish or your customers are stupid is also not a good look for a CEO trying to keep a business together. Gerald Ratner made an infamous speech to the Institute of Directors in London in 1991,[1] where he described the quality of some of his products as 'crap'. The subsequent crash of his company – and himself – just shows that a try-too-hard style in public speaking takes people so far, but if the content's crap itself, it'll take you so far out the door that it's not funny. And that was in an analogue reporting age. And he'd even rehearsed it. You either need to have your own inbuilt critical faculties or not be so arrogant and scary that you can't ask for honest advice from someone else.

Talking heads

I've had a mixed history of public speaking. I included that ancient Greek Pericles example when I was asked to do a TEDx speech a few years ago at the Houses of Parliament in London. At the time, I was slightly nervous of speaking without a lectern and with absolutely no notes – and it's a feature of TED talks that people tend to wear those head mikes and stride around the stage. Do watch the spoof of how to deliver a TED talk (digg.com/video/ted-talk-parody.) It made me feel slightly better anyway.

For various reasons, the period leading up to the speech was one of the busiest in business I can remember (and yes, I know it sounds like a pathetic excuse... because it is). I had very little time to prepare and rehearse, and I was speaking on a new topic for me – it was about 'Re-branding Democracy'. Stupidly, I thought I'd give cue cards a go. These might work for some people, but best not to try them for the first time in front of a big audience at a televised event.

Suffice to say that I got the cue cards muddled up, forgot my thread and was basically not very good. Sadly, it's still one of the main video features that appear when people Google me. I'd really like to wipe it and do it again, because now I love those head mikes! I love to stride around the stage! I've trained myself not to need notes (most of the time anyway)!

You see, the key is... *practice*.

Actually, I'll modify that. There are a lot of people who, whether from natural confidence, learned confidence from their parents or peers, or expensive confidence from attending a well-known school, seem to have the knack. And then, it's about making sure you have something interesting to say and polishing it up.

I'll even modify that 'something interesting to say', by the way. Whether we like it or not, when it comes to public speaking, delivery still trumps content. Research varies, but allegedly around 93 per cent of people's impressions from a speech are gained from body language and tone of voice, and only around 7 per cent from what is actually said.[2] That might sound depressing and superficial, but it's human nature and it's probably a good idea to work with it.

It certainly took a long time for me to get that into my head. After doing a bit of stage stuff as a child, mainly dancing, but also school plays, by the time I got to adolescence, I suddenly discovered extreme self-consciousness, and extreme stage fright of anything that felt like acting or public speaking. This continued through university and early career, where my voice would squeak and my hands would visibly shake when I had to do anything like a presentation. If it's anything like that for you, it's a bad idea to hold a piece of paper or point to anything on a chart as this is a dead give-away of nerves.

To try and get over this, I used to write out every word that I wanted to say, and, worse still, then proceed to read it all out in the actual presentation. The words might even have been interesting, but with my head down, mumbling and shaking, my audience were probably running through their to-do list in their heads, doodling or something equally gripping, whilst they prayed for it to end. In those days, there was obviously no such thing as a smartphone, where you might pretend you were looking something up, or tweeting. Over the years, I graduated to being able to glimpse up from my written notes from time to time, and try and remember to smile occasionally too.

It took a slightly brutal intervention by a senior female executive to make any significant improvement. I am still in her debt, and didn't fully appreciate just how unusual she was to be a woman in such a senior role at the time – although the price she felt she had to pay in those days was to have to play-act like a male executive and not to have children.

We were pitching for a really important and prestigious piece of business, and I was supposed to be presenting the strategy. True to form, I had written out my script.

When we were rehearsing, she watched me and said, in slight horror, 'You're not intending to read that aloud, are you?'

I went red, mumbled something about how important I felt it was to get the words right.

She lurched forward, grabbed my notes, and said, 'Look, you know it, it's really good stuff, and you don't need these notes.'

And do you know, I didn't.

After an initial panic about not being able to memorize everything I'd written, and a bit of a burble, I managed to say something that vaguely reflected what I knew.

And, to actually look at people while I said it rather than bury my head in my notes.

The lesson for me (and one that I have had to relearn many times over) is that speeches and presentations don't have to be a memory test, that you will NEVER remember all the detail and nuances of exactly what you want to say, but that if you've really thought about the main narrative line, can recall a few facts and phrases, and can look at the audience with confidence and ideally with some decent visuals, you can usually get by.

After various courses and even more dud speeches over the years, I got better, and thought I might share with you the most useful lessons. It goes without saying that these will be no substitute for the vast number of excellent books and professional training sessions about 'How to Do a Speech'. Public speaking is an important skill for getting on in the world and wielding influence on things you care about.

To be clear, I am not advocating that you need to be a 'grand performer' or cabaret artist to be a good speaker. You don't even have to be an extrovert. Some of the most compelling speakers are the quiet ones, who recognize the power of silence. But you do have to conquer your inner voice that says you can't do it and replace it with something else.

KNOW WHO YOU'RE DEALING WITH

I was asked to speak at a senior executive dinner by a high-profile chairman, and he asked me to comment on what was happening in the world of branding, and what implications there might be for this group of people; they represented the board of an international travel trade association. My excuse, which will sound familiar by this stage, was that I was exceptionally busy leading up to the session, taking client calls right up until my arrival, and I hadn't had time to check the backgrounds of the attendees.

Starting the over-dinner speech and warming to my subject, I launched into some passing, and slightly critical observations of Nokia, who had recently sold their handsets/phones business to Microsoft for (relatively speaking) next to nothing. A few years before, they had been valued as one of the world's leading brands, so quite a come-down. I had never directly worked for Nokia, but my comments on the reasons for its downfall were based on some well-established research by leading academics. What I had failed to check was that one of the guests had not only worked at Nokia, but had also had the brand responsibility in his remit. My 'remarks' didn't go unchallenged. Inevitably, he was both defensive and aggressive, and the interchange was slightly embarrassing for the other guests all round. If I'd have realized the Nokia connection, I would still have mentioned it, but would probably have 'shaped' my comments better.

Say what?

If I had any other overall rules/guidelines/bitter and sweet lessons after doing a few thousand presentations in my life, varying from the excruciating to the well received, via a fair amount of mediocrity, they would be:

Prepping

- Your speech needs a clear point with a beginning, middle and end.
- The worst speeches I've made are those that combine a bit of reading aloud with a lack of a clear point. Even if you deliver this to your audience in a breezy/covering over the cracks/faux confident style, you won't fool people.
- Know your audience. Know what might annoy them.
- Structure is important and will keep you focused.

- Know who's on the receiving end, and what they might be interested in. Make a list and group them into three themes.
- What is it that you know that you can uniquely bring that might help and interest them? List those alongside.
- Get in the shower and think about your introductory gambit to make people think they're going to hear something useful (eg 'Today I'm hoping to show how to achieve x, y and z' or 'This presentation will capture all the latest advice on how to stop worrying, make a lot of money and never have to do work you don't like again.' And so on. I like things in threes. Three is good. Three is a magical number. Quite apart from anything else, I can just about remember three things.

Writing it

- Your intro should set up what you want to say and get people paying attention because it sounds as if it could be so very relevant.
- Assemble your evidence and examples into three sections that develop and support your story. Try to use visuals, quotes and quirks to illustrate it and prompt you to make the right points.
- Make your presentation charts bullet-point-free zones. (PS I don't have a maximum number of charts for presentations. You can use some as momentary glimpses, others just to act as interesting backdrop placeholders. But you're supposed to be the main event as speaker. Not the charts.)

- Use as many 'personal business' stories and anecdotes as you can.
- Be careful of using examples of companies that you haven't worked with, haven't researched properly, or if there's a danger someone in the audience knows them inside out and may want to make a point.
- Make sure any charts are nicely produced, by you or a friendly designer. And absolutely no errors allowed. Spelling mistakes give off the impression that other things may not have been checked properly, or might be inaccurate.
- Make sure you know what the story arc and links are.
- Make sure you have at least one or two sight-bites or sound-bites that capture the key thoughts and ideally help people remember.

Rehearsing and delivering

- Try to memorise your opening sentences. They need to reassure the audience that you're going to be a good, confident speaker and that you've spent some time considering what they'll find interesting and can nick at a later date.
- Stand and deliver (or walk around purposefully if better). Make it feel like a conversation rather than a proclamation.
- If things are flagging, do a 'hands up' question (eg who thinks that Apple will still be a leading brand in five years? Who doesn't?) This can sometimes wake people up.
- End with something like 'So, what I hope to leave you with are these three thoughts/questions/prompts.'
- Await thunderous applause.

- If there's a Q&A session, try to answer crisply and in a relaxed way. I have droned on far too long, far too many times and people switch off and wish they hadn't asked.
- Say thank you. That's it.
- Go and network, obviously after taking lots of cards for all those business prospects you're (hopefully) going to get.

DON'T MAKE A SPEECH, PUT ON A SHOW

Sometimes, if you're confident enough in front of the right audience, it can work better to break with convention. One of the speeches I remember was by the then creative director at Saatchi & Saatchi, Paul Arden, who was responsible for some of the most memorable campaigns in British advertising history. I don't use the word genius lightly, but he was one. Curious, principled, batty, ageless.

He was giving a speech to the whole of Saatchi, and wanted to emphasize the importance of bravery and creativity. He found speaking a bit tricky – he was actually rather shy, and a visual ideas man; check out his brilliant books such as *It's Not How Good You Are, It's How Good You Want To Be* and *Whatever You Think, Think The Opposite*. It became part of his personal brand that he said less and showed more. This time, though, he started to read out what felt like a more conventional speech, in his halting style. He then stopped, and started at the beginning again. At first, we all thought he had made a mistake, but then it became clear that That Was The Point. Bravery and creativity was so important in that business, that it stood being said all over again. It might seem a bit of an affectation in these cynical times, but we did pay more attention the second time, and remembered it. Other examples of his speeches were when he had a naked man stand next to him, and a time a cellist played for the whole of his speech time while he stood there. As he would say, 'Don't make a speech, put on a show'.

This worked in a creative business, but obviously might not go down as well at a bank.

Body language

I am sure you have your own favourite Disney films. One of mine is *The Little Mermaid*, and particularly the bits with Ursula, the sea witch. I know that the story behind this is cruel, sad and problematic; Ariel, the mermaid, is willing to give up everything – her voice, her home, her mermaid's tail – to persuade a man to fall in love with her. It's not great role-modelling for young girls and women.

However, my biggest laugh-out-loud moment is when Ursula is trying to persuade Ariel to give up her beautiful voice in return for being given legs. At one point, Ursula is explaining that being unable to speak isn't necessarily a huge problem. As she turns and walks away, she says '...and don't underestimate the importance of... BODY LANGUAGE,' as she simultaneously waggles her not inconsiderable rear.

She's not wrong there. Particularly when it comes to presenting in public. As I mentioned, over half of people's impressions are from body language. It's worth trying to consciously manage this – and actually, I find it gives you confidence. I am not talking about that ridiculous legs-planted-apart-look which is supposed to make you look 'strong', and mannered hand movements that supposedly look 'confident'. Frankly, it can make people look as though they're trying to speak at a pyramid selling conference.

It's good to find your own way.

What I noticed in the early days of speaking on stage was that I would sometimes cross my legs over and flap my hands when they weren't shaking in a distracting way. The crossed-over legs looked closed and coy, as though I didn't really want to be there (I didn't, most of the time, it's true). The flapping hands looked nervous and irritating and were distracting. I saw all this for myself when I was filmed for the first time on a course. I was horrified as well as grudgingly grateful.

One of the few things I gleaned from self-help books was about how useful it could be to visualize yourself in the way you want to come across, before you start speaking. So run a video in your mind's eye about what you should ideally look like and sound like when you're speaking. (The books often then say you should touch a pressure point on your wrist or something, to fix that image in your mind, so that you can summon that feeling back at a later date. It works for some.) This might sound strange but it has been really useful – and is a technique used by athletes who visualize running the race and winning at the other end. It obviously can't work for all of them, but you know what I mean. I have used this technique to make sure my head is in the right central position to look more confident rather than inclined to one side, which looks apologetic, and that my shoulders are straight as opposed to hunched nervously – this helps with voice too. I also use steady hand gestures and start off evenly balanced on two feet (without The Splay). It's also good to think of the expression you'd ideally want to see on your face, and the cadence and pace of how you want to set the tone.

Just breathe

I have found breathing is quite useful too. Both generally, and Big Conscious Breathing.

I don't know whether you're into yoga or not, but in addition to the usual postures, what it taught me was about how to do deep upside-down breathing. You slowly breathe into your stomach first, then inflate your chest, then back the other way. It's easier than it sounds once you're used to it, and is essentially like the 'diaphragm versus just chest' breathing that lots of practitioners and presenters talk about.

In case it's useful, I have also found this type of breathing quite useful to get to sleep in stressful times, particularly if you are consciously able to empty your head at the same time.

One of the benefits of Big Breaths is that it doesn't just make you feel calmer before going 'on stage' (any stage, big presentation or small meeting), but it also has advantages for another fundamental thing about speaking...

The voice

I confess that I enjoy those reality TV programmes that feature well-known (or even has-been) singers transforming their voices, whether from pop star to opera star or soap star to theatre star. It just shows how versatile the voice is, and how much it can be managed and consciously controlled. Clearly, we're all going to have a 'natural' range that's our default voice, but even that can be tuned and shaped with a bit of work and practice. Of course, actors do it all the time, to enable us to see them in different characters in any given role.

What I obviously don't mean is anything like the old elocution or received pronunciation type of shaping and training. One of the better things about our changing society has been the acceptance and celebration of diverse accents, backgrounds and styles of speech.

The most famous and noticeable 'voice transformation' in public life was former British Prime Minister Margaret Thatcher. Listening to recordings of her when she was first in politics as opposed to her 'Iron Lady' era is remarkable. In the 1970s, if you were aiming to be a 'strong leader' in what had been a man's world, her advisers reasoned, well, you needed to have a strong voice to go with that. For a woman at the time, that meant having a deeper, more powerful and more resonant tone that would feel more confident and authoritative. The result was much lampooned in political satire, but was, from her point of view, very effective. 'Soon the hectoring tones of the housewife gave way to softer notes,' wrote her biographer Charles Moore, 'and a smoothness that seldom cracked except under extreme provocation.' And yes, I found this infuriating and patronizing too.

Research has shown people's preference for lower-pitched leaders, a preference so strong as to swing elections. I am not suggesting that 'going deep' is the right answer in every case, male or female, but there is a practical challenge that women tell me they feel in particular. Which is making yourself heard if you have a naturally softer, higher voice, and also projecting enough confidence through your voice. Many times I have seen real potential in young women, but for whatever reason, they told me that they worried about it being difficult or potentially unappealing to strengthen their voice. Clearly, society should accept that there are many routes to power and influence that sound different, but social science research tells us that we're quite a way off yet.[3]

I used to suffer from 'nervy high voice' syndrome in speeches; once you start off a talk in a higher register, it's difficult to get down from there, and you can get stuck in that upper monotone. When you're nervous, your throat muscles tense and your pitch rises. I got a voice coach to help me in the end. She had trained as a singer and actor, but had also coached people in places like law firms (all that advocacy needed a persuasive rather than an irritating voice). She did that deep-breathy thing with me ('chest versus head' voice), and voice pitching and throwing exercises. It taught me to consciously think about the starting voice pitch.

The eyes have it

Confident speakers have a steady gaze. Good eye control. I am not sure how many people do this naturally, but ever since I had it pointed out on a formal training course, I've noticed the huge difference it can make in any meeting and speaking situation. You may notice some people glancing around the room whilst speaking, looking quickly from face to face. If you're not careful, that can look nervous and as though you're trying to seek approval from everyone; you might well be, but it's not a good look. One of the most useful presentation training sessions I had was when I was advised to count to four before I moved from one face to another. This might sound slightly stagey and weird, and you need to count silently to yourself, but actually, it helps you get into a more confident rhythm of speaking. Also, if you focus on one face at a time, it helps you feel a better connection with your audience and come across as more conversational rather than declaiming over the heads of a faceless mass.

EYE EYE IN PRESENTATIONS

Glancing upwards should only be for deliberate use – ie when you're trying to make a slightly stagey point, or if you want to come across as a slightly batty creative genius or dreamy character.

Glancing to the side is usually a bad idea because it can make you look shifty, as though you have lost concentration or are telling an untruth. This is obviously not the same as giving side-eye, which has its theatrical uses.

Looking downwards to think before answering questions is better for authority and can be quite handy for collecting your thoughts or stealing a sneaky view of your notes and prompts.

Shut up and drive

Another thing I have noticed about good speakers is that they use the sound of... silence.

They use this in two main ways. First, to let the words breathe a bit (as well as yourself). It's so tempting to gabble and try and get it over with when you're nervous. Second, if you've deliberately said something that you hope will be a bit funny and are hoping people might laugh – well, stop for a bit and let them. Speaking to a larger audience usually means a delayed reaction and the last thing you want to do is start talking again before they've had a chance to get the joke.

This latter thing, though, is also a test of nerves. There's a reason why comedians like to test their material on small audiences before they make a fool of themselves on a big stage. Saying something, pausing for a laugh and then getting tumbleweed is a sad and lonely thing.

I have a story about this tightrope that still makes me wake up in the night.

I was asked to do a vote of thanks to a very high-profile CEO, who was doing a speech at a business dinner. He was interesting and professional, and talked a lot about the strengths and meaning of 'Their Brand'.

In explaining the research work that they'd done to understand and articulate what the brand stood for, he paused for effect, and then said, 'Our brand is about being... *Red, Rock-solid and Restless*'.

The Three 'Rs'.

I swallowed.

When it came to my vote of thanks, I obviously thanked him for a very good speech, said we loved it when he talked brand to us and… that, as far as '*Red, Rock-solid and Restless*' was concerned, well… 'That always does it for me.'

You may have needed to be there, but as soon as those suggestive words left my mouth, there was a stunned silence in the audience.

One woman even gasped.

I thought to myself, 'I've really gone too far this time.'

It may only have been a second, but felt like minutes later, that the audience finally erupted into laughter and then applause.

It was a relief to say the least.

I wouldn't recommend sailing quite so close to the wind. I knew how close I'd come when the organizer dropped me a note the next day thanking me for the 'memorable' vote of thanks. He said, 'It was a terrific, if risky', speech.

In other words, it almost certainly went too far.

Even though a few people still mention it years later, I wouldn't recommend going too far unless you have the hide of a rhino, bullet-proof nerves and convenient amnesia.

I have none of these.

But, it doesn't negate the need for pause at certain points when you speak. Just best rehearse what you'll say – perhaps with an objective friend to warn you when something's going to fall flat or get you fired.

In the end, it's all about… timing. Give it time.

Look Mum, I'm on TV

If you fancy a career as a commentator or pundit, or you are even just asked to appear on TV (or do any media stuff), my bits of advice are:

a   the answer is yes, now what's the question; and

b   be a great producer of content/ideas/research/examples/ angles.

Having some kind of media profile is a great way of enhancing your 'personal brand' value, whatever you do.

I say 'say yes' because the major channels have such tight deadlines that, by the time you have mulled over whether you have got anything to say, whether you might deign to say anything, whether you can bother to get out of bed at dawn and/or re-arrange that drink you had fixed with friends, the news channels will have moved on to someone else.

You've got to put yourself out for these kinds of opportunities. And believe me, if the news topic is anything at all that might be relevant to anything you might know, you can usually find a way to connect it to your point of view about the world/business/whatever:

- Whatever happens, you just need to think about what the viewer is going to see and hear from you and what impression they're going to get (again, they're the real audience).
- Think of, write down and rehearse a few phrases or interesting sound-bites that you think might be broadly relevant to the topic and help you or your organization's agenda.

- Don't get too hung up on the individual interviewer and their questions. I hesitate to say that it can be quite a good idea to do the politicians' interview wheeze, which is to say something like (to any question they don't want to answer, or for a point of view they want to get across at all costs), 'Well, that's obviously a very good question, and the simple answer is xyz. But the most important thing here is… [fill in your own/blank party line].'
- You can then shape the interview a bit if you're lucky, and use it to promote your profile and point of view.
- Try seeing yourself as others might see you on the screen (and perhaps on the sofa). A bit like when you're doing public speaking.
- Visualize your body language, your manner, how you might be engaging in what you're saying.
- There are three of you in this relationship, and the most important person is the viewer.

As well as trying to get the mainstream media channels to give you airtime, obviously you can produce content yourself and get it out there – at minimal cost these days (and if you do or say something sufficiently interesting, it may well be picked up more broadly, of course). The same principles apply, though. Think of who you're doing it for, and what they might need to see and feel as a result of seeing you. Arrange yourself and your features accordingly.

And finally…

Last thought on this speaking thing, and conquering nerves.

You often don't conquer them.

One of the best and wittiest speakers I have ever heard (who is now well into his 90s) confesses he often throws up before a speech. He's still that nervous. That's lifelong learning for you. Use your worries and nerves as drives to prepare. Ironically, it's often those who worry and bother more that make the biggest strides.

And as for 'That Voice' you might have inside saying you can't do it/it's too terrifying/you're an imposter. Well, try turning its volume down, putting it into a Donald Duck-type silly squeaky voice you can laugh at.

Or alternatively, tell it to go and screw itself.

NOTES TO SELF

- You have got to get good at public speaking. Yes, really.

- Form usually trumps content, whether we like it or not. Stand, look, breathe, pitch your voice right in your mind's eye and ear.

- Use the nerves and adrenaline. Or there's always Rescue Remedy.

CHAPTER EIGHT

Extending skills and expanding life

On how to add some good strings to your professional life – and an honest take on personal stuff

I was seven when I became obsessed with a BBC TV programme called *The World About Us*. It's ancient history now, but my obsession with the presenter lives on to this day. More recently, he was slightly inappropriately described as the sexiest octogenarian going.

This presenter is, of course, Sir David Attenborough.

In the old days, he would wear khaki shorts and stride around rainforests, sit with mountain gorillas and generally be the planet-whisperer for me. The programme showed just enough of the nasty stuff that startled a young girl (me) and a generation into crying and caring.

I bawled my eyes out as I watched a beautiful, vast and long-living rainforest tree being power-sawed down to clear land for humans.

How could people do this to such an amazing living thing? And what about the poor animals and wildlife that lived in it? Where would they go?

At the age of seven I didn't have much of a grasp of the subtleties of geopolitics, corruption and the effects of abject poverty on human preoccupations. Obviously, if a family has a choice between eating to survive and conserving a tree, then the tree, however amazing, is going to go.

Even if my perspective has become nuanced over the years, that angst and upset never left me, and the environment has been a bit of a life thing for me.

Quite apart from the personal interest, what I have found really gratifying is the power of 'having a thing' in life generally, that may or may not be connected to the day job. When I was at university, it never occurred to me that you could have a career attached to the environment.

Why have 'a thing'? Well, having a thing in life generally means that you always have something that lights you up, is a channel for your passion, and doesn't feel like work. You may or may not be lucky enough to make it the centre of your working life but it will have hard and soft benefits.

The thing about things...

Here's the thing about a thing. It can help your career and extend your sphere of influence in unexpected and wonderful ways.

Whilst I went into the commercial world of advertising, I retained my interest in the environment, stayed a member of WWF and Greenpeace and continued to be locked to the television whenever David Attenborough appeared.

For the first few years of working, I came to realize that my views on the environment were:

a a bit weird for most because they were ahead of their time, at that time;

b boring a lot of people, who had other goals such as getting seriously rich, or going to parties;

c not exactly compatible with making and selling lots of stuff in the conventional sense.

I still possess a wonderfully patronizing letter from one of my early clients in advertising. They made intimate paper products such as toilet paper and sanitary towels and had a large and dirty footprint. At the grand old age of 25 in the mid-1980s, I summoned up the courage to write to the senior marketing director to say that all the evidence showed that the environment was becoming a significant issue for business and government, and that they should be planning to change to keep on top. The reply was perfectly nice but missed the point. He spoke of how the environment was a niche issue (although, of course, it only affects the whole of humanity and the natural world in its entirety – *D'oh!*), that his company was mainstream and so had no plans to do anything radical. But that, of course, they would monitor the situation, and so on, and so on.

You know those films about environmental (or any) apocalypse, when the nasty politician and/or corporate executive is the first to die a horrible death from the meteor strike/tsunami/nuclear blast/reconstituted dinosaur? I had a few fantasies like that but decided that it might be better to change things to get even.

Help came from an unlikely source in 1988 when, completely out of the blue, Margaret Thatcher gave a speech to the Royal Society, where she said that the environment and climate change were crucial issues for mankind and needed to be addressed.

Suddenly, I became the most popular girl in school, or rather, at Saatchi & Saatchi. There I was, an advertising executive who knew lots about the environment, which was exactly what clients wanted to know about. I set up the Green Unit, where I was supposed to advise clients. I will draw a veil over the lack of popularity of my advice at the time, which was that companies actually needed to DO something about environmental protection if they wanted to advertise it. I found myself fighting a tide of greenwashing, with companies desperate to say something, ANYTHING, that might in any way show their customers that they were responsible and so green. Let's just say there were a lot of weasel words, accompanied by visuals of babies, rabbits, trees and globes.

Making waves as an insider

Whilst that was a frustrating period, two things happened. First, I managed to make quite a few conference speeches about the importance of the environment to consumers and therefore that businesses needed to act. Second, I got to meet all sorts of people who were movers and shakers in the environmental movement, whom I tried to help and work with in various capacities over time. I was invited to sit on various government eco-advisory boards, the Sustainable Development Commission, and the boards of WWF and other environmental organizations. Of course, this was mainly pro bono stuff, but it both fulfilled 'that thing' again, and also gave me extra strings to my brand bow.

I also learned that sometimes, to make the biggest difference, it can help being on the inside of business rather than as a pressure group on the outside. I was able to sneak in all sorts of research and 'corporate responsibility' change programmes under corporate cover using the language of business. It was much easier than camping outside a nuclear power station or lying down in front of diggers.

Nowadays, the environment and sustainability are becoming properly embedded into mainstream business strategy, and a lot of governmental policy too. Partly due to right-thinking people and customer/citizen demands, but also, let's face it, because the insurance and investment industry see big, dirty and polluting businesses as a bit of a risk. Who knew?

We've still got a long way to go to ensure that we don't all choke, fry or obliterate the planet, but it's work in progress.

And yes, all this stuff even eventually got me to meet David Attenborough in person.

Now, whenever people say to me that, yes, the environment's important, but actually, THE most important thing for them is poverty/education/preventable diseases and so on, I would relay the words of a one-time mayor of Mexico City. True, he was dealing with some pretty severe pollution problems as Mexico City sits in a bowl of surrounding mountains with a cloud cover lid, and so is in danger of getting poisoned or boiled in that pot. He said something like, 'If we don't get the environmental thing sorted out, there won't be any other issues left to worry about.'

Now, I'm not going to argue with you about which comes first, the Armageddon chicken or the toxic egg, but you get my drift.

Making good use of your thing

You can extend your experience and skills, as well as motivation, by having that Extra Thing in your life, whatever that might be. Whether or not it relates to the paid job you do every day, it will show anyone who cares to look that you are an interesting person, that you have experienced different organizations and challenges beyond the usual. In particular you may be able to get experience of sitting on, or advising, a board and doing things such as corporate governance well before you get a chance to do this formally in a main job, or bigger organization. Whilst corporate governance might sound like something to chant when you're suffering from insomnia (and it can feel like it too), it's important to know what it is and how to do it in order to climb up the corporate pole, as well as helping you avoid any accidental fines or jail sentences if and when you run your own organization.

It's a good idea to accept invitations to join advisory boards on your chosen 'thing', or offer your services free to a charity, a social enterprise, a start-up or whatever, in an area that reflects your extra-curricular interest. It rounds you out as a person, as an executive, and can make you stand out and be even more desirable as a senior employee. Most organizations are interested in presenting good corporate responsibility these days, and some are even doing something about it. A few are making being fundamentally 'good for society' central to what they do as a business every day. Hallelujah.

And you never know. That 'extra-curricular' thing might turn into an enterprise idea at some point.

It's a wide world

It may be that my experience in sustainability was also a helpful factor in being considered for board positions. You are valuable not just for what you can do, but also how it looks to the outside world. Happily, some stakeholders like to see broader and nicer interests on board member CVs or resumés.

Having a foot in two camps – one in the commercial or for-profit sector, and one in the charitable or not-for-profit sector – can sometimes make you feel awkward because of their differing priorities, but I think that there are a few things it's useful to remember:

a the politics and stresses of the charity/public sector can sometimes make the commercial sector look like playtime;

b not all angels work in the charity and public sector;

c not all evil people work in the commercial sector.

I gave my time pro bono for six years on a charity board. Over that time, they lost almost half their funding due to government cutbacks, and we had to 'restructure' the organization, which is usually a euphemism for having to close sites and make people redundant. Unfortunately, it was true in this case and sadly necessary if the charity was going to survive. It involved some horrible and nigh-on impossible decisions about who to make redundant and how to use scarce resources to keep the boat afloat at all – it had a lot of beneficiaries who would have been left bereft if the charity had gone under. It was a really upsetting period for all.

Fast forward a couple of years, and I was up for re-election on a different company board. One day on Twitter, I noticed that someone had written that it had given him great pleasure to cast his vote against me. As it happened, 97 per cent of the voters didn't agree with him, but I always believe in trying to engage with people to find out what their problem might be. Anyway, this person directly messaged me, saying that he blamed me and the board (note, not the government turning off funds, not the financial crisis, no, it was all our fault apparently) for the fact that he lost his job, that he hadn't been able to find another and he said that he was someone who bore a grudge. Clearly, I sympathized with his situation, but tried to explain that it was quite hurtful to see such an unpleasant tweet on a completely unrelated organization when I and the rest of the board had given our time for nothing to the charity for six years in order to help people. There was no reply, and I guess I should have ignored the comment in a dignified way – the poor tweeter had probably only wanted to let off steam. However, I do think it's important to tell people that, in an ordinary, human kind of way, you do mind about casual insults.

Sweet nothings in the non-profit sector

I have loved the non-profit boards I've done, but just remember that it's not all hearts and flowers. Most charities have to look at themselves like businesses, to make best use of funds and perhaps ironically, lots of businesses are now seeing themselves as purpose-driven enterprises, trying to solve global problems in a decent and sustainable way. For years, I hobbled along with one foot in each camp. And now, the two are sort of blending and blurring into each other.

HOW TO HELP A NON-BUSINESS, AS A BUSINESS PERSON

You can make a contribution to non-profit and public-sector organizations in lots of ways and get a sense of reward back too:

- Help them think about their 'customers' in the broadest sense (ie their funders, their members, their employees, the media), what it is that connects with those audiences and help them get more influence and raise more money.

- As an outsider, you can spot the opportunities that people on the inside might not see any more.

- It gives you the experience of working with tight budgets, working with people who have very different motivations from those in business, learning about sitting on a main board, the language and practices of corporate governance and important things like safeguarding, and having enough financial reserves to keep the show on the road.

- Helping non-profits find a vivid way of expressing what their purpose and mission is, how it would affect people's real lives and what they can do about it and how it can be done without it costing too much.

- It's also often a good way to understand how governments work (or don't).

This conversation about non-profit versus the corporate world reminds me of a call I once took from a young woman who was doing some fundraising for my old university college. I listened politely as she went through the introductions, the background chat, asked me what I did, making it clear she had no idea of what I did and hadn't tried to find out, all of which was obviously a long preamble to the 'how much money are you asking for' question.

Having got that out of the way, I then asked her what she was intending to do when she graduated. She breezily said, 'Well, I was originally thinking about going into marketing, but then I decided I would be more interested in doing something good…'. I did some deep breathing to absorb the insult, and then advised her as nicely as I could on things such as marketing actually being quite useful to help charities thrive, not just the commercial sector, and that marketing was also quite useful to make sure that people got the kind of products and services they needed, whether in the public or private sector. I don't know if it was lost on her, but it certainly made me feel a lot better. But here's the business lesson, whether you're working in the commercial or charity sector: if you're asking anyone for money, it's best to know a bit about the person you're asking and to 'market' to them appropriately.

On boarding

There's another more 'conventional' thing that it's possible to do to extend your experience at certain stages in your career. That's to become a non-executive director. This is about sitting on the main boards of organizations in a part-time capacity, and as an independent, responsible adviser, albeit with legal responsibility, as opposed to an executive with operational responsibilities.

There's some really quite good progress that's been made about getting more women on main boards; the global average is just over 20 per cent, and it's 10 per cent or below in South America and Asia, going up to 30 per cent in the UK and even pushing to 40 per cent and beyond in France and Scandinavia. The more pressing problem is with female CEOs and on executive teams, where the percentages are still woeful.

The non-executive job is basically a combination of therapy and policing. Your job is to oversee, support and challenge the senior executives who run the company every day. It can be really interesting stuff, and some senior executives 'retire' into this kind of plural existence, sitting on a few boards and dispensing wise advice. It sounds fabulous, but can be a bit nerve-wracking and time-consuming when a company is a takeover target, has a corporate scandal, is facing some kind of international fraud or cyber-attack. Because YOU are legally responsible for ensuring that the governance and systems (and people) of the organization are up to it and doing the right thing! So, it's not an easy retirement home. Personally, I've really enjoyed it, and have got to sit on the boards of a great range of organizations from banking to fashion, electrical retail to healthcare, media to music.

HOW TO GET A NON-EXECUTIVE DIRECTORSHIP

There are limited paid opportunities like this, and you tend to get approached about them by head-hunters. This is because there aren't that many roles going, and you do tend to have to have very senior experience on boards, governance, finance and so on, but it's always useful to sign up for non-executive director courses and 'do good network'. It's nice and interesting work if you can get it, and the best way to get it is to be as successful and well-perceived as you can be in your core working life.

One of the things I tried to perfect when I started these board positions was a facial expression that was intended to give off the 'ah, yes, I know what you're talking about' impression. I realized quite early on that, no matter how many courses and seminars I'd been on, there was no short-circuiting having actually been through it, said it and done it. You'll be amazed at what you actually do know, however unconsciously, as opposed to what you are convinced that you don't know. However, this doesn't necessarily apply to the range of acronyms and jargon every business and industry gets to use.

Don't be disheartened, and don't feel you need totally to assimilate. Part of your value as a non-executive director is to be there as an independent 'uncontaminated' person, to stop conventional groupthink and ask the big stupid questions such as 'remind me how this is going to make money/ be good for our customers/be motivating for our staff'. Of course, you can fully indulge your imposter persona if you choose, but it gets much easier with age and practice, and when you gain confidence that you're not a complete idiot for asking the more obvious stuff. Like most boards, one of the frustrations is thinking, 'I wonder whether to ask xyz, or whether I'd look stupid'... and then for someone else at the other end of the table (the odds are that it will be a man, as men still significantly outnumber women on boards) to ask exactly the same question. You live and learn, and that's the point, of course.

On the big stupid question thing, I remember being on a retail board, and I don't think I'm betraying any secrets to say that traditional retailers used to be a very particular breed. The business of running shops was addictive and complex, and it was easy to get obsessed with logistics, product and price. I was shocked at how little attention customer issues got around the board table. I felt strongly that the business had to ask the right questions, like 'How are people changing the way they live their lives, what do they *really* need from this category, and how can we provide the best way for them to get that?'

The answer wasn't always traditional shops. These businesses have been disrupted by the online world. From time to time, you have to put up with being patronized by people who know a lot about the details of the category, but have become blind to outside forces. You need to know enough about the category to frame your questions in the right way, and make suggestions. But if you see something, you need to stick to your guns. Ideally in a peaceable way.

The final thing about extending and stretching your experience is that it gives you what corporate and coaching jargon describes as 'optionality'. Otherwise known as not having all your eggs in one basket. It's really good to know that, from these wider experiences, you can 'pivot' in your career as and when you might need, and extending your contacts helps too. In the end, it can be fun to wear a few hats. And if you're naturally as paranoid as me, it's a good thing to feel you're spreading your career risk in case anything goes south.

If some of the above are ways of extending yourself, your brand and your possibilities, there are things you can do closer to your core Mastermind topic that can also work wonders.

The joys and pains of writing books

Writing a book is good. In fact, if you're going to build your personal brand and be known for something, it's a great way of setting out your stall and your agenda on something you feel strongly about and might be able to be famous for. Or if you work for a bigger company and can persuade them that it/your enhanced profile would be good publicity for them too, they could subsidize its production, and guarantee to buy some copies.

But you do need a decent idea. Obviously, my own 'work' brand has been partly based on branding, and I have done a couple of books on the subject. The first, *The Future of Brands*[1] involved interviewing 25 high-profile people around the world on what it would take to be a world-leading brand in 25 years, starting from the Millennium. The content gave me lots to talk about for years. Similarly, doing a book for *The Economist* was interesting in its own right and helpful in positioning 'brand' as a proper and hard economic asset.

I'll be honest and confess that getting a book done can be torture if you're also working full-time, and you can say goodbye to any free time for at least a year. You are the party pooper on holiday sitting in the dark and looking pasty when others are having a great time.

But, as we know, no pain, no gain. The people who end up running organizations are those that bother to put themselves out, and put themselves out there. It all feels worthwhile when you touch the book (it can obviously be digital only, but for some reason, a physical thing feels more rewarding than a joyless e-reader), and you can then wear it round your neck for posterity. A few other thoughts:

- If you can't manage to do a book, then offer to write a chapter of a book for someone else in your industry.

- Or, perhaps create a booklet that your company can use for marketing and PR.
- If you can't manage that, write an article.
- If you can't manage that, a blog, or post stuff up on LinkedIn.
- If you can't manage that, hopefully you can manage 140 (or even the new 280) characters of tweet, or to post some suitable pics that show what an interesting/intelligent/ glamorous/kindly/ambitious (in a good way) brand you are on Instagram.

Personally, I keep Facebook to personal information only, and have abandoned it regularly when the 'liking' becomes too much of an extra duty. But the line blurs for so many businesses, which I guess is a good thing in the 'important to humanize business' kind of way.

The important thing is that the stuff you do and say is true to you in some way. In a digital age, and in trying to build an effective personal brand, it's not a good look to be exposed for fibbing about the stuff you're liking or selling.

Doing all this 'extra' extending to your core can be a really good investment, and it also reflects one of the characteristics that a well-known CEO said was important to being a good leader. That you need to be 'hyperactive' in some way. A bit of a hypertasker.

And this level of energy will also stand you in good stead for another stage of expanding your personal assets if and when you get pregnant at some point.

Expanding your life… with children

Jacinda Ardern, New Zealand Prime Minister, said, 'I am not the first woman to multi-task. I am not the first woman to work and have a baby – there are many women who have done this before.'[2] I've talked a bit about this already in Chapter 2, but I'm going to look at how having children can enhance who you are and what you do at work, even if it doesn't feel like that at the time. I'm going to be doing this with rather raw honesty, so please feel free to look away now and rejoin me for the next chapter.

I am claiming absolutely no special knowledge of the 'I don't know how she does it' type stuff. I often didn't feel like I was 'doing it' at all.

Certainly not consciously. My children are now no longer children except, of course, they are, because I still suffer from the 'how to infantilize your grown-up children' syndrome.

I'm going to split this into two oh-so-subtle camps:

1 the difficult things;
2 the good things.

Again, if you haven't got any children yet and/or aren't thinking about having any ever either, you may want give the following section a miss. Also, I am very clear that everything I'm about to say is a privileged problem. I take my hat and everything else off in homage to all those women and couples whose lives are infinitely more difficult on scarce resources.

The difficult things...

The obvious insight is that it can be bloody tiring being a mother. But there are a few other things I can think of that fit in the 'not so rosy' stuff:

- Getting pregnant in the first place when you're both working full-time. Or, a lot of my friends who've been through IVF tell me of how surreptitious they need to be about jabbing themselves, sneaking off to get tests or get implanted, all the while feeling awful and not wanting to tell anyone in case it doesn't work.

- Not wanting or being able to tell people that you're pregnant during the first three months, because, well you want to wait until 12 weeks. Worrying every day that something horrible may happen and pretending to drink alcohol when at work or friends' gatherings because you don't want to give the game away, even if you're usually a very enthusiastic participant. And horrible morning sickness, again at a time when you don't want people to know.

- Still trying to score all those goals at work and look presentable/speak coherently/look totally committed whilst juggling all these hidden baby balls.

- Getting fed up of people touching you and asking when it's due and how you're feeling, tiptoeing around asking you any questions about what you're going to do after the birth (in case they land up in HR hot water). Getting fed up with the limited range of clothes you can wear, with your thickening ankles and occasional brain fade.

- Generally feeling overweight and unattractive.
- Feeling irrationally irritated that men don't go through any of this.
- Worrying about the niceties/nasties of maternity/paternity leave, how long you can afford to take off, and how on earth you're going to manage childcare between you when both sets of grandparents live inconveniently on the other side of the country, are not in the country at all, or have sadly already shuffled off this mortal coil.
- How it is that nannies seem to have a much better set of perks than you do? Reading the latest tabloid scare stories about violent child-minders and/or whether you are permanently damaging your child's well-being and future prospects by not being there every minute of the day yourself. Whether you will need to spend all your salary on childcare and whether it's all worth it.
- Whether to confess to considering going part-time before you absolutely have to tell people and wondering why that should matter anyway.
- Worrying about whether the birth will be painful, writing your birth plan and attending NCT or prenatal support classes (if and when you can get away from work in time) and worrying they're just a little bit smug.
- Working even harder in the final few months just in case anyone thinks you might be slacking or don't have your mind on the job. Trying to make sure that everything is up to date and neatly handed over and hoping that no one will find out whilst you are on maternity leave about the various mistakes you've been secretly hiding.

- Wanting and planning to have whale music/spa-type tinkly music to accompany your birth, practising your breathing and blowing... and then ending up asking for a mallet over the head when it's too painful.
- A lot of crying, crying, crying (and that's just you). Hating your partner for not waking up (or pretending not to) at any time of the night. Being angry that they can't change nappies like you do. Just hating your partner generally (it's probably mutual at this time).
- Being in your dressing gown for weeks. Not getting out of the house except in hours of darkness.
- Putting on a false 'it's all fine' voice when taking calls from the office.
- Agonizing about when to go back to work. Biology says one thing, brain another. Trying to keep the peace with both. Feeling that you should welcome your partner taking just as much of the childcare strain, and yet somehow wanting your baby to want you more.
- Finding and keeping hold of a great child-minder/nursery/nanny (yet more management challenges, in addition to the paid day job).
- When you return to work, worrying constantly about whether you've left your precious bundle with a psychopath. Catastrophic fantasies about ghastly things that could go wrong. All the time.
- Having a constant source of bickering and loathing between you and your partner (if you're still together). Who's doing more, whose turn is it. Whose meeting or job is more important.
- Peeling your crying infant off you on countless occasions.

- Worrying about signing up for nursery schools. Worrying about signing up for any schools. Worrying about whether they're going to make friends. Worrying about whether they're invited to as many parties as the other children. Worrying about whether the entertainer you've booked for your child's birthday party is going to be any good or a bit strange. Getting slightly sozzled at said parties. Worrying about whether you look OK in comparison to the mothers who are married to invest-ment bankers and do a lot of Pilates. Worrying about being late for everything, and whether your children will ever forgive you or end up being on a psychiatrist's couch because you were late to hear them sing *Some-where Over the Rainbow* as a solo (cue more crying...).
- Forgetting most of your child's school friends' names (and their parents). NB: This is a never-ending story, even well past university.
- Worrying about whether 'helping a bit with homework' can actually mean you doing it yourself.
- Hating all the creeping and ingratiating stuff you do with the headmaster/mistress to help your child get into the next school.
- Thinking that your child is spending too much time on various things from social media to television and per-sonal appearances, and not being quite sure how to tackle this. Trying to keep a steady, nonchalant but sup-portive voice when you're asking tactfully about this.
- Worrying about whether it's being a bad parent when you start to enjoy a few weekends just with your part-ner again.

- Worrying about whether they're getting in with the wrong crowd at university and wondering how many of your friends might be able to help provide some work experience/internships, and whether that's cheating.
- Worrying about whether anyone is going to pay your child, who isn't really a child any more, to do a proper job at some point. Is that the right thing for them? Will it make them happy and fulfilled? And what about their future?
- Will they meet the right partner? Will they get married and if so, will you want to make a speech?
- If they have their own children, will they want you to do some childcare? The circle of life spins around...

But of course, if you don't yet have children, don't let all this put you off.

The good things...

Running a company? In comparison, a piece of cake:

- If you can survive the above lists, you've got it made. You become an experienced hypertasker and hyperworrier.
- If you didn't grasp before how to persuade people to do things they don't want to do, you will be amazed by how much you understand everyone's inner six-year-old – and have a bigger range of tools like suggestion/cajoling/distraction/competition to deal with it. And only reach for the nuclear 'command' button if there's an impending emergency.
- It rounds you out (in more ways than one if you're not careful – I know). It's truly mind-expanding (if you can find the extension leads when you need them).

- Also, despite all the worries, seeing your children become decent, caring, responsible human beings is indescribable.

I had two daughters whilst working and when asked in an honesty session whether they felt short-changed by me not being there enough during their childhood, my children told me that, of course they missed having their mummy around more, in contrast to many of the other children. But frankly, they had wonderful nannies who have become like big sisters to them, and having me at home would probably have been pretty stressful anyway. And, actually, they were really rather proud of me. This was incredibly heart-warming and also made a change from feeling the usual embarrassment that every mother gets from just breathing near their teenage children.

And as far as knowledge and wisdom transfer is concerned, you know you're getting somewhere when your child gives a favourable critique of your management style in dealing with a teenage misdemeanour. I'm sure that she won't mind me mentioning it, but one of my daughters in her teenage years fibbed about going to bed while we were on holiday, sneaked out to a club with her friends, and then they accidentally locked themselves out so had to call me at 4 am to be let in. According to her, I used the 'more from sorrow than from anger' management-type approach really well in my disappointment and worry. She felt really bad and guilty as opposed to angry and resentful.

Having children, if you do have them, will be part of who you are, and what you have experienced. Then it's down to you how you use that experience to grow yourself.

Although some of my comments above are obviously slightly light-hearted, combining children and work is viewed differently now except, of course, by certain elements of the media. Western workplaces at least have had to become more aware of fairness and sometimes litigation. There's more understanding, more flexibility, more balance, more sharing of the responsibilities. And a big recognition that these relate to both women and men. And also both partners in same-sex relationships.

It's important to be the same 'personal brand' in essence when you are expecting or have produced the baby goods at work, as who you were before. By that I mean, when you announce to senior colleagues that you're expecting a baby, it's good to present it in your usual professional manner.

While your boss(es) may outwardly pretend that they're thrilled with the news, and personally they may well be, you can bet your bottom dollar that inside they're screaming and thinking things like 'what the hell are we going to do, how are we going to cover and what about all the logistics?' After all, whatever the size of company, they will need to carry on doing business and making money or at least not losing money in order to pay for everything and everybody's benefits. That means you too.

So, perhaps consider saying stuff like, 'Look, basically the baby's due on such and such a date. I'm intending to come back x months/years later. This is what's likely to be happening while I'm away and this is how I'd suggest we cover over that period. And I'll obviously try and be available for advice if needed.'

Do your own version according to the needs of your business.

And in the end, doing a bit of personal brand extension into children can potentially make you an even better, more understanding, more empathetic, more capable, more human potential leader.

NOTES TO SELF

- Get/do 'That Thing' which really lights you up, whether as part of (or additional to) the day job.

- Wherever possible, actively use it to broaden your life/ working experience too.

- Do the extra stuff that gets you noticed.

- Having children can be both wonderful and tricky. Appreciate the many ways it will grow you as a person.

CHAPTER NINE

Women rule OK

*On how to 'do leading' in a way that suits you...
and helps others*

In case it hasn't been completely obvious, I want more women to be running organizations. A lot more women. Whether it's big or small, public or private, Fortune/S&P/FTSE or your own business.

There's lots of statistics to choose from, and here are a few. Just 4 per cent of CEO roles and 11 per cent of CFOs globally are women (so basically, all the people with control of the money).[1,2] In 2018, white women held almost one-third of all management positions; this compared to just 6.2 per cent Latino women, 3.8 per cent black women and 2.4 per cent Asian women.[3] Meanwhile, nearly half of all Indian women drop out of the workplace as junior or mid-level managers.[4]

On start-ups in the UK, for every £1 of venture capital investment, less than 1p goes to all-female-led teams, according to a report by the British Business Bank.[5]

Also on start-up businesses, companies with female founders only attracted about 2 per cent of total venture funds (which is ironic considering those businesses have been demonstrated to perform better, with less risk).

According to BCG's analysis, start-ups founded or co-founded by women performed *better* than male-founded start-ups. Despite being comparatively underfunded[6] – and by a large margin – these businesses generated 10 per cent more in cumulative revenue over a five-year period: $730,000 compared with $662,000 for the average male-led start-up.[7]

And, of course, the same principles apply to governments and global institutions.

The world needs more women in charge, quite apart from anything else. Ideally, I'd prefer nations not to be constantly threatening each other with nuclear obliteration, bullying trade wars and genocide. And it seems that most men – especially younger guys – seem to feel the same way. Of course, that's not to say women can't and won't be tough. Biological mix just makes a difference in the way we deal with each other.

Take New Zealand's prime minister, Jacinda Ardern's response to terrorism following the Christchurch terror attacks in March 2019. She wore a headscarf to comfort mourners, asked Donald Trump to provide Muslim communities with 'sympathy and love' in the wake of the attacks and rallied support for the Christchurch Call, which calls for tech companies to police their online platforms.

It sometimes feels hard to look beyond the typical alpha males of the world in political leadership, but thank goodness for the 'niceness' that is Ardern. She hugs people! She speaks like a human! She's strong! She makes things happen! She says things like this:

> One of the criticisms I've faced over the years is that I'm not aggressive enough or assertive enough, or maybe somehow, because I'm empathetic, it means I'm weak. I totally rebel against that. I refuse to believe that you cannot be both compassionate and strong.[8]

> Getting stopped in the middle of the lingerie section, when you're trying to stock up on a few things, by an older man who wants a selfie is a little bit awkward... but I don't let that get in the way of me trying to do normal things, because that is when I get to interact with people as well. Preferably not amongst the underwear, though.[9]

There's just the small matter of *how* we get more women in charge. And what we can all do to do our bit. And stop getting in our own way sometimes (when others have already been doing a pretty good job of that for us).

So, a few thoughts, to add to the sum of many others about getting up that greasy pole and staying there. I am aware I'm standing on the shoulders of a few women giants here. We have covered how your imposter can ironically be quite a useful drive to achieve things, providing you don't pass any of your own pain on to others. Academics have also shown that you can use some level of anxiety in a positive way and turn it into a powerful force in your life.[10]

I'm going to be looking at what you personally can do in three ways to help get more women up and running more organizations. That is, what you can do for yourself, how you can help others, and how you can influence current systems.

How to help ourselves

In 2015 there was the fabulous and award-winning ad campaign 'Like A Girl' for the sanitary product brand Always. You may well have seen it. While women, men and boys behaved in a silly and self-deprecating way when asked to do something 'like a girl', young girls themselves ran and tried as hard as they could with confidence and pride – they had not yet been influenced by 'the social rules' that can unhelpfully define womanhood. For them, doing it 'like a girl' meant doing it as well as they possibly could.

It highlights what an insult the 'like a girl' term has become, and how limiting and reducing it can be for girls' perception of their talent and power. And how insidious it can be on their prospects to lead and succeed.

For years and years, every time my senior director asked to put a 'cup of tea' chat in the diary, I was convinced that I was going to get a telling-off and/or get fired. Again, I guess that this kind of anxiety and drive, that old fear of failure and being an imposter was quite a propulsion. For a girl, of course.

One of the most infuriating pieces of feedback on my performance as an executive I ever got was when my (male) boss at the time said I was doing well and ran a great team, but that I needed to develop more 'stature and gravitas' if I wanted to go further into senior management. In particular, he said I could sometimes come across as being a bit of a 'breathless girl'.

I seethed and sulked.

I felt humiliated and patronized.

I may even have felt like hitting something if I hadn't (very annoyingly) felt like crying.

And yet I think one of the reasons I felt so angry and hurt was that, deep down, I thought he had a point.

From time to time, I could come across as a bit too keen. It wasn't so much that I needed to 'lean in', but I actually needed to 'lean back', and look wise and grown up.

In fact, it was one of the best pieces of executive advice and feedback I got. I did improve and was grudgingly grateful. I have even told him since. He had forgotten and was nonplussed that it was so significant.

However, I still didn't feel that I improved enough, and I felt there were clearly some inner issues that kept surfacing in an unhelpful way. That somehow, in business, I secretly felt the need for a 'strong man' executive to approve me.

A grown-up. A man. To be in charge. To make the final decisions. After all, what did me and my imposter know in comparison?

I don't think we need much pop psychology to know where that might have come from. Many women have told me that they could share parallel couches.

Later, of course, you discover that you know just as much, and are capable of doing at least as much, as any man. And, the stats would say, do it better at least 50 per cent of the time. We just need to step forward and to the front.

Cheering on the role models

Back in 2015 there was a really catchy song called *Cheerleader* recorded by a Jamaican singer Omi. I often used to find myself singing along to it, and then I started paying more attention to the words.

To paraphrase the lyrics, he was singing about how he had found himself a 'cheerleader' in his girlfriend. That she was always there when needed, 'in his corner'.

I've got nothing against cheerleaders, but they are not the main event.

I want women to be the leaders, not just the ones cheering (mainly male) leaders on from the sidelines.

I came very close to 'settling' on several occasions. Settling for supporting executive roles to the main event rather than taking them up myself. The forever-deputy danger stakes. Two stick in my mind.

By some miracle (as I saw it back then), I had progressed to deputy strategy director at Saatchi & Saatchi. The head of department was a woman who was also a great role model and mentor. She had always been very supportive, even and particularly as I got pregnant twice on her leadership watch. She had no children herself, was a strong feminist and took no prisoners. The other all-male members of the executive team seemed rather scared of her and behaved like naughty schoolboys behind her back.

When my children were both little, I started to feel that something had to give. I had huge and very demanding clients, was travelling a lot and feeling like an absent mother as well as feeling that I was doing a less than brilliant job at work. I had more or less decided to ask for eight weeks holiday and/or go part-time. In those days, that meant you were firmly on the 'mommy track', as they called it. I discussed it with my partner (now my husband) and he was as supportive as ever. Although he was honest enough to say that this would probably mean I'd got as far as I was going.

I started saying to my female boss that I needed to discuss a different or shorter working week, longer holidays or whatever. Her face clouded slightly. 'Mmm. I do understand the pressures, but if were you, I don't think I'd mention that to the CEO at the moment.'

It turned out that she herself was planning to take a year out to travel the world.

She was going to recommend to the CEO that I take over the department and become strategy director. Nowadays, I may have argued that I could do both a shorter week *and* do the lead role, but those days were not nowadays and I was not then as I am now.

I duly shut up about the 'shorter time' request and became strategy director, running a sizeable team. Obviously, it involved lots of hard work, but I was able to shape and develop the team and its culture in a way that I found truly satisfying. And funnily enough, being in charge, even if not of the whole company, meant that you could be more in charge of your own time. And enable others to work differently too. You can lead in a way that helps move everything forward.

One of the fabulous women in my team later said that, because I was running the team, and had two children, it never occurred to her that she couldn't and wouldn't do both. She went on to run some really important businesses as well as her children.

A note on slightly less conventional role models – and it's always good to have them. I have a vivid memory of the singer, songwriter and rapper Neneh Cherry – the mother of the current pop star Mabel – performing on the UK chart show *Top of the Pops* in tight Lycra when she was eight months' pregnant in the 1980s.

She rocked the look, and it was the first time I properly realized that you could carry on as normal while pregnant. As a woman in business, never ever underestimate the power of role models and the part you can play (even if it's unintended).

And now for the news

What I also learned about my first major elevation to a leadership role was the importance of managing your news proactively when you're in a relatively high-profile industry role. When I told one company that I was leaving to take up another role, the timing was rather inconvenient for them and they weren't best pleased – in fact, they were keen to play down any impact. Before I knew it, I had an industry journalist on the phone, saying she had been told I was leaving and was 'giving me the chance to comment'! That's the usual code for 'we think you may have been fired'.

As it happened, I had been sworn to secrecy by my new company until the following week. I didn't feel I could break confidentiality and tell the journalist where I was going, so just said that, 'I was leaving for a senior job in a related industry'. This wasn't sufficiently specific, so I duly got a headline on the front page of the industry magazine, major-ing on the fact that I was leaving – and describing me as an agency 'veteran'. I was 39! I know that I had been there for 10 years, but really… . It also featured one of the worst pro-fessional photos I can remember having taken – and which I thought I had managed to have destroyed – with big bags under my eyes from baby-and-travel-interrupted nights and looking 'serious'. For which read glum. Not sure where they got the photo from, but I could have a guess… .

The article and photo even prompted a reaction from a friendly head-hunter, who called the next day and asked me if I needed a job, because 'my girl, it looked as though you might have been fired'.

Thanks. So, it wasn't just me being paranoid.

In hindsight, I should probably have done a bit more proactive reputation management. For example:

a Consciously built relationships with industry journalists. I hadn't really seen that as a key role as strategy director, but if you want to run something at some point, get on it.

b Told the journalist off the record where I was going as CEO and promised to give lots more detail as soon as I could. One of the great things about social media, of course, is that you can now get direct messages out to share. But someone might still beat you to it or the right people may not see your social feeds, so good to get commentators on board.

Shortly afterwards, a similar thing happened to a well-known senior marketer who was leaving his post, and the opening words of the front page article included 'X, who is *not thought to have another job to go to…'*. Well, he clearly recognized how that 'code' would look to the readers (this euphemistic 'code' includes terms such as 'their role will not be replaced'), because the next day he dropped a note to all his marketing acquaintances explaining that he had not, in fact, been fired. And that he was actually leaving the country as part of a long-planned and long-billed project to start a new business.

What IS it about human beings that they sometimes want to believe the worst, not the best about a situation? And, in fact, gain some kind of satisfaction thinking that even clever and important people screw up sometimes? Is it a bit of the 'There but for the grace of God go I' syndrome? I guess it fits into the classic definition of *Schadenfreude* (ie pleasure derived by someone from another person's misfortune). More lyrically nasty, perhaps, is the following old (allegedly) Chinese proverb, 'Nothing brings as much pleasure as to see a good friend fall from a high roof.' I hate this kind of thinking. A conscious effort to change this tone would make a real difference to a more positive social and business environment, as well as people's mental health. Let's stop feeding fear and loathing.

The week after my glum front cover, the happy 'new news' about my real CEO job was out, and the same publication featured it on page 5 rather than the front page as before. A bit annoying, but I lived and learned. And actually, used my crossness to go into the new job with a lot of energy, and to prove a point.

Saying cheese

It's a good idea to get some decent photographs done. I know this sounds a bit vain, but if you don't actively use and distribute these, people will pick whatever detritus they can find from their old files or Google images. Sometimes, of course, you can't help this. When a popular newspaper did a profile on me, they happened to feature something I had said to Sir Martin Sorrell at a dinner a couple of years previously. It was actually a very nice article overall, but the picture they used in the paper version of the article was even worse than the one in the industry magazine. You just have to try and drown out the stuff on Google images with quantities of the stuff you like.

TIPTOEING THROUGH REPUTATION BOOBY TRAPS

Bearing in mind that bad things are going to happen at various points in your working life:

- **Option 1:** Grow a very thick skin, ignore all nasty comments, possibly sticking your fingers in your ears and singing at the same time and/or meditating your way through by rising above outrage and ascending to a higher plain of consciousness. This particularly suits people who have no problem with self-confidence and don't care what others think. I don't know too many people like that. Particularly not women. However much 'personal development' work we do.

- **Option 2:** Try and feed the 'positive beast' from the other direction as an insurance policy (this applies to

---

companies as well as individuals, of course). Perhaps have your own website/book/column/blog/social profile etc. Manage some of your own image and contacts independently, not just through your main job and firm, who will have their own agenda. These days, it's easier to manage reputation if you've built up a decent online and social following. NB: This does come with health warnings – if you say ANYTHING that ANYONE might be in ANY WAY annoyed about, you've got to pop your proverbial tin hat on.

As a postscript, in a subsequent discussion with another female CEO who stepped down from a very high-profile job after 10 years, she advised me that, 'Whenever you say you are leaving something, *always* say that you are joining something. Whatever that might be.' I remembered those wise words, although I probably went a bit too far and took on so many plural board roles, laying too many eggs in too many proverbial baskets, that I was run ragged for a while.

You see, even when you're supposedly 'up there' in leadership terms, you can always give yourself a hard time about how hard it's going to be stay up here. And before you start to think that, frankly, you may as well just give up, nip off and get a low-profile job, go freelance, do subsistence farming or similar, well, all of that brings its own stresses.

One of the great benefits and privileges of doing what I do is to work with and get to talk to a whole range of business leaders, and also (not always a happy privilege) to see how other people lead at close quarters.

So, here are some of my thoughts and observations on leadership, and how to try to get and stay up there if you want to. These are both from a personal perspective, and based on what I have gathered from a wide range of female leaders too.

1. Don't take the 'be yourself' thing too literally

I know it's personal development/coaching wisdom to talk about 'being yourself'. And I know, and also say myself, all that stuff about 'you'll never be as good at being someone else'.

However, whilst I'm all for honesty and authenticity, there are some aspects to 'being yourself' that are frankly the rather unappealing bits of what Freud described as our 'id'; the part of our personality structure that houses our rather basic and unedited human desires. Being a functioning human being in society means getting most of your 'id' and some of 'yourself' under control, and then it's just a matter of degree.

People might say they find it fun when you've had a few drinks with the team and have let your hair down a bit. But it can be very difficult for people to get any dodgy images and inappropriate memories out of their minds afterwards and look at you as a leader they can respect.

Whilst it's helpful to be honest about what you're good and not so good at (to encourage people to think about their own performance and how they can improve – and also give them permission to give you honest feedback), you don't want to hand over all the bullets to a very large gun that you can be executed with later. Maybe one blank bullet at a time, and ideally with the intention of helping other people be better rather than just for your own catharsis.

For example, saying, 'I tended to be a procrastinator myself when I was younger, and it got in my way – I had to force myself to go on courses to learn how to "do it now". I think that would help you too.'

You can run but you can't hide from yourself. Just try to make sure it's your best self wherever possible.

You need to sort your personal issues out so that you can make them work in a positive way for yourself and for others.

Perhaps get yourself on some personal development/ coaching courses (see Chapter 5). They will be a good investment.

2. It helps to stand out a bit

Ideally, you want to have something like a 'unique selling proposition' for yourself. I really hate that term; it sounds like a slug of old US business jargon, because it is. But the United States has still got more globally successful, valuable brands than any other country. By far. So, there's clearly still something in it.

Stand out for the right things. It's a competitive world out there, whether we like it or not. Stay on the side of interesting and memorable as opposed to being weird and unforgettable. Particularly when you want to lead things. Running stuff requires some self-awareness and self-control.

Standing out can mean having a memorable trademark, that symbolizes whatever you do and whoever you are that's a bit different. Perhaps not something as obvious as a bow tie equivalent. And also something that can be updated and renewed. You might be good at hats or glasses, for example. Or being funny in a particular way. Or serious and profound. Or always having interesting statistics, distinctive quotes. It's a bit like novelists who have a distinctive style you know you're going to enjoy.

Emotional and intellectual consistency is good, providing it doesn't become boring. Better for your teams that they don't have to deal with Jekyll and Hyde unpredictability. That can be debilitating and draining.

I stumbled on a podcast, *Business Jazz,* with an Irish business coach, which mentioned me. The podcast guests were discussing leadership, and to my everlasting flattery mentioned strong personal brand approaches he'd observed like Steve Jobs... and me! I hasten to add that it was in the context of wearing distinctive clothing styles at work. He actually said that I was known for wearing (the same) black Chanel-type dresses and consistent jewellery. This was very interesting, particularly as I don't own – and have never owned – any Chanel dresses at all and I never actually wear any jewellery (apart from one eternity ring that looks like a plain wedding band). But it was certainly weird and instructive hearing myself discussed as a third person.

I'm never quite sure whether some of my other 'distinctions' have worked for or against me, but they were certainly authentic. Apart from my support for the environment from an early stage, I have always been interested in complementary therapy and personal development. Anyway, I remember when we were moving into a new office, and I got someone to do a Feng Shui analysis to make sure we didn't unwittingly drain away all our wealth. And to make sure we had a warm 'flow' through the building for our people and guests. You may be thinking I've totally lost it at this point but honestly, it was worth the cost. If nothing else, it highlighted that the main entrance to the office building faced north, and would be in danger of feeling cold and unwelcoming. They suggested we had a fireplace or something... and so we did. I remember the poor building manager trying to understand what this was all about, but actually, the 'warming up' of the reception area made rational sense as well as lending a 'woowoo' feeling. None of us would think this Feng Shui was weird in somewhere like Hong Kong, just good practice. We created a very nice fireplace, we got lots of compliments, and things generally went OK for a while. You see, that's one of the benefits of being CEO. People have to humour you.

It stood out, anyway. And, seemingly, so did I, with my 'new age leadership' ideas... .

3. People need to want to work with you

There are, sadly, still quite a lot of leaders who even now feel that you can bully your way into getting people to do what you want, and that it's actually more effective. The statistics on all this stuff are compelling, but so are the qualitative examples. I've talked about Glassdoor, and what it reveals about the internal company world, in an earlier chapter. And 'bully' has become a very expensive word from a personnel department and general company reputation point of view. It's a well-known risk factor, and studies have demonstrated time after time that having an over-domineering CEO is a main risk factor to the whole enterprise because they won't tolerate challenge, and also don't get the best out of people.

If you don't want to see people be or become brilliant, you don't have the right to call yourself a decent leader. All those clichés apply about recruiting people who are going to be better than you. I can't understand why not everyone gets that – after all, if they're good, they're going to make you and the company look good too. And yet some people can't resist trying to make everyone else look and feel smaller so they look bigger.

The other annoying hobby horse is when people somehow view nurturing as a 'soft' quality. Try telling that to the natural world, where the female of the species is often deadlier than the male. Nurturing is one of the most powerful forces in nature. You can love people to death.

And, in business terms, if you love your people, they will tend to love your customers a bit better.

Even if you're not yet a leader, it's a good idea to make sure that people want to work with you. To attract the best people to your team, you need to have the strongest, most exciting vision thing going on, to be having the most fun – and ideally be one of the people that others in the organization can see is going places.

You may have met people in life who could be described as either 'radiators' or 'drains'. The former are people who light rooms up, who see the possibilities in things, and generally try and make things and people better.

'Drains' are those people who get everyone down in the weeds of 'can't', sucking all the air and vitality out of a room so that people can't breathe. Get them help, or get them out.

I don't want to confuse radiators with 'Pollyannas'. (If you don't recognize the term 'Pollyanna' by the way, she was a character in a famous American children's novel, basically an irrepressible optimist who was determined to find good in everything, however desperate the situation.) Whilst you want positive people, you don't need too many fantasists in denial.

Aim to be a radiator, not a drain.

4. People won't like you all the time

This is one I struggled with, perhaps because I have a bit of the inner Pollyanna, but also because I'd ideally like people to feel happy and fulfilled all the time. That tends not to be a permanent part of real life or the human condition.

And in any organization, any business, any government and public-sector role, there will need to be some difficult decisions that people won't like.

For example, I can't remember any of my executive colleagues ever saying to me, 'Do you know, my team could do with a real budget reduction or salary cut or fewer resources next year.' Everybody inevitably asks for more – and more than is available to go round. You will have to juggle priorities, egos, feelings, stakeholders, financials and your conscience. And some people are just not going to like it. All you can do is explain, lay out the plan, paint a picture of the future that you hope they want to be part of and encourage people to get on.

Moving from being a 'therapist-leader' or 'lead-nurturer' to 'sometime executioner' is tough.

Another thing I struggled with is that People Do Leave. It took me so long not to take it so personally; in fact, I still haven't quite got over these types of emotions. The way I tried to articulate it to myself after a while was:

a   if they just wanted to go and do something else in life, then that was sort of understandable (one woman only left my team to fulfil a lifelong dream to join the circus – not much you can do apart from pack their trunk…); or

b   if there was a career/salary roadblock that I couldn't fix without seriously disrupting the rest of the organization, then sadly, that was that.

Incidentally, none of the 'tough stuff' is an excuse for being badly behaved or unpleasant. Ever. You need to be the grown-up. People will just sometimes need to see you and even hate you as a business parent and you need to command a bit of respect – even one with flaws.

Just to reiterate from an earlier chapter. Try not to forget people's names and try not to get people's titles and name spelling wrong when you write to them. They get upset. I remember a male chairman once who constantly confused my name with another female member on the board. I was insulted and outraged… until I did it myself. Not just with women, of course. Just generally. Just apologize. It's a frailty of the ageing brain/attention overload/digital dementia/whatever. No excuse not to keep on trying to get these things right though (and there are 'memory techniques' to help, which associate people's names and characteristics with memorable images).

5. There's no getting away from working hard

I'm constantly asked about work/life balance, and I see and hear it being asked all the time. I understand the question, but I find it a bit frustrating.

Work/life balance is not really the same as work/family balance. Work/life balance sounds as though work is something that you need to get through, and then you can live your life. But we can spend a lot of our life at work, whether we like it or not, so it's part of life.

Trying to find the cause and importance in what you do is a worthwhile endeavour, whatever business or issue you're involved with, whether commercial or not. It's not as impossible as it sounds. I remember working with a ball-bearing manufacturer once. I can honestly say I have rarely worked with a set of people who have had a greater sense of purpose. The way they saw it was that they kept the world moving, so they'd better do it brilliantly. They were infectious. In a good way.

Clearly, your children (and sometimes, even your partner) need you, and they may not be very amused by having to come into the office all the time, either physically or metaphorically. I get it.

But honestly, if you want to run or start a company, or be at the top of your game in the work area of life, it's difficult to get away from the need to put the hours in – wherever and however you might do them.

That can obviously be during the hours of daylight, but it can also be after the children are in bed, or up a mountain when you have ideas. There are lots of encouraging signs about the fluidity and flexibility of workplaces these days. Ones that suit both parents as well as people who prefer their own space. Work based on outcomes and results rather than being locked in an office.

It's not hours-ism for the sake of it. Thinking about the Malcolm Gladwell book *The Outliers*, you have to get a

LOVE YOUR IMPOSTER

lot of practice to be really great at something – 10,000 hours, apparently. I know so many people who are talented and appealing, but for whatever reason, they've never applied themselves enough.

I had a great PA once. She was very bright and helped me hugely with my working life by recognizing and compensating for the things I wasn't good at. She didn't sneer at organizing meetings and sorting my to-do list. She was so good that when there was a vacancy for an account manager, I recommended her. To cut a long story short she ended up being a board director at Saatchi & Saatchi. I could not have been more proud.

In contrast, another assistant was always telling her boss that she didn't really want to be a PA, and that she had aspirations for more. Meeting rooms weren't booked, the coffee was late and there were always excuses for stuff not being done. She didn't get promoted.

6. No, people won't 'just notice' if you're doing a great job: Get your value into your head and heart

Frankly, it's outrageous that I'm even mentioning this, because, in comparison to many colleagues, I have been a failure at negotiating my own salary and packages over the years. I have often managed to act as though I'm grateful, if not also surprised, that anyone might give me a raise. I don't think this necessarily garners respect, and frankly, when there are hard decisions to be made about how to distribute available money, then if you're the one who doesn't make a fuss, sadly people will often go down that path of least resistance.

So don't listen to me on this one. Read Sheryl Sandberg's advice in *Lean In*, on how she stopped 'negotiating like a girl'. Or otherwise, any success I've had in trying to be more assertive has been down to the help of a coach, who actually helped write a 'script' for my next salary review. The 'coached' script goes something like:

> In thinking about what the organization needs to deliver next year, this [example of xyz success] is the kind of value I'm bringing, and it's appropriate for the business that I should be rewarded in a way that reflects that. It's also clearly important from the business' point of view that I feel properly valued and motivated to bring even more.

I am sure you will have your own version or will be able to develop one.

Alternatively, you may feel like me, which is that if I have enough money to take care of my children, have a decent home, buy some clothes I like and go on a decent holiday, then I'm OK. It's also a lot more than so many other people have. I don't feel the need for a yacht, a Ferrari, or whatever. Money is not the main thing that turns me on. But it's nice to have some, and negotiating will always be part of working life.

Sometimes, people are just too busy and/or preoccupied to notice what you've been doing and whether you're truly doing a good job. Don't bother to get upset or angry, you just need to make it a bit easier for them to notice – and particularly if you have a more 'subtle' way of achieving change and results in your management style rather than making a big show of it. It never ceases to amaze me how people can be seduced by those who talk and gesture a lot, but don't actually manage to deliver.

You may not like, or may not have a habit of, 'copying people in' to your successes and achievements but honestly, just do it on the important stuff. You don't want to keep chirping up that you've solved the equivalent of the work sock drawer, but if your team has been awarded something, had some great customer comments, or you've been invited to present at a major conference, then it's good to let people know.

I remember in one management role, in an appraisal, my CEO boss at the time commented that he felt I could be more visible on new business and handling clients. The fact that I had managed and helped my terrific team to do just that and with great success had been lost on him. In fact, we had huge successes in winning new business as a team, in industry awards, brilliant new people joining and getting rave reviews from clients. He just hadn't directly associated all that with what I may have done. It's funny when your natural instinct might be to give credit to others and take the blame yourself. It sometimes works that people notice that it was you doing what you do. But it doesn't work so well, particularly when you are owned by US companies who probably quite rightly tend to be much more upfront about this stuff.

7. You've got to be prepared to be 'on it', all the time

It sometimes makes me feel tired even talking about this, but all my experience with world-beating, hugely valuable brands of every persuasion leads me to realize that the long-term successful ones keep up a constant level of energy, renewal and innovation.

On the 'personal brand leadership' front, Madonna was always the ultimate practitioner on this with her constant re-invention. You may not feel the need to go as far as Miley Cyrus in her transformation from wholesome Hannah Montana to being naked on a wrecking ball... but it was certainly a very profitable re-invention of its type.

So, what can one do to re-invent as more of a mortal? Well, ideally not get stuck into too much of a time warp on the appearance front; whether we like it or not, people are still heavily influenced by your sense of currency in personal presentation. And, good to attend conferences, courses and keeping working with lots of new, young, entrepreneurial people to make sure you keep up to date with industry news and tech developments. I've had to force myself to go onto certain social media channels to see what they're like, but you do learn something. Try to update your smartphone or devices so you don't embarrass yourself, unless you are making a deliberate retro statement on an old-fashioned mobile. But do make sure people know it's deliberate, and even why.

Keep on doing and learning things that stretch and extend you – perhaps do a lateral arabesque into a different industry to use your transferable skills to make a fresh impact.

And read, and travel, and ask people questions.

The minute you feel you know everything, that you've seen everything and that you've got nothing more to learn means you'll fossilize and become less and less relevant and less and less valuable to any organization. Clearly, there may be some stages in your life where you don't much care about that… but that's for then, and this is now. I was recently at a seminar on Artificial Intelligence, where some of the attendees were business people in their 70s and 80s, there because they were still curious and wanted to learn.

And (note to self, as much as anyone else) try and do a decent amount of exercise, so you move well and fluently for as long as you can.

Staying up that greasy leadership pole takes a bit of stamina and energy.

But, a lot more people are capable of leadership than they may think they are.

And not like a girl. Like a woman.

Women running things needs #YouToo.

NOTES TO SELF

- Take (fair) feedback, use any cross-ness, and step forward to lead stuff.

- Best to try and be your 'best self' as much of the time as possible.

- Develop and use some kind of distinguishing feature/attributes to make you stand out.

- Love people (even knowing that they won't love you back all the time); be tough/do tough love when you need to.

- Stay on it. The world needs you…

Bonus quiz! 'Are you ready for leadership?'

1 Do you have a pulse? Yes/no
2 Are you good at something? Yes/no
3 Have you ever been able to persuade someone to do something they don't want to do? Yes/no
4 Are you willing to learn new things you don't know about? Yes/no
5 Can you add up? Yes/no
6 Can you grit your teeth and stick to doing stuff when you want to crawl into a corner and cry? Yes/no
7 Are you willing to get therapy/do personal development stuff to sort out any shit that might get in your way? Yes/no

If you got more than a couple of yesses, it's worth giving it a go...

CHAPTER TEN

Nice guys don't finish last

On why the business and wider world really needs niceness to work

If there's one thing that's guaranteed to get me going, it's when people quote that whole 'nice guys finish last' line. You may already know its origin, but there's some doubt as to what Leo Durocher (a legendary baseball player and manager of the Brooklyn Dodgers) actually said. Apparently, it was 'finish seventh'. I'm not sure that equated to last, and it doesn't have such a final and damning ring to it. But what's not in doubt about Durocher is that he really believed that nice guys don't come first. By the time he got round to writing his autobiography some years later, and had appropriated the 'finish last' quote as the truth, he went further and said:

> Nice guys. Finish last... Give me some scratching, diving hungry ballplayers who came to kill you... That's the kind of guy I want playing for me.

Yes, he was quite the guy.

Two things to note here:

1 it's about a particular North American ball game (not life); and
2 he said it in 1946.

But so memorable was the quote, and supposedly so 'easy' to apply to wider examples in a clichéd and macho business world that it's stuck way beyond its sell-by date.

And whilst you can still run a company in that old-fashioned way (and even secretly believe the 'nasty guys win' thing might be true), the digital world and hashtag social movements make it much harder to apply.

The days when people could hide dastardly activity, when businessmen (because it mainly was men) dressed and spoke like macho stuffed shirts and the few women there were felt they needed to wear stilettoes and padded shoulders to compete are no more. No, if you're going to be a bastard these days, you need to be either oblivious or confident that you can get away with it in plain sight. Then it's up to customers and regulators on whether they're going to let you get away with it.

We can all think of 'hall of shame' figures in business who are disreputable, misogynistic and unsavoury to be around, but the sobering truth is, people have to be pretty damn bad (or corrupt, in a way that rips off customers and scares investors) and their critics very determined in order to put people off buying what they find convenient. It's all very well telling market researchers that you're outraged about someone's behaviour in business, or that sweet independent high-street retailers are closing, but if you don't actually change your own behaviour and 'vote' the nasties out (even if the 'nasties' haven't done anything illegal), then you're part of the problem.

What was interesting about my time at Saatchi & Saatchi was that the culture was actually very emotionally engaged, intense and supportive, in that 'love/hate' family way. The vision was truly extraordinary and for the most part, I loved it. The thing I could never reconcile myself to, and that I could never say with a straight face (or indeed, at all) was that the agency believed obsessively in 'winning' (that was OK)... and that part of that was their belief in enjoying seeing 'other people lose' (not really OK). Why would you want to feel that, let alone say it? I just couldn't see why it was necessary, but perhaps that was just my bleeding-heart liberal self speaking.

Being the best

Actually, a quick incidental story on that bleeding-heart liberal thing, and finding nice surprises where you least expect them. My agency was invited to pitch for the British Army advertising account some years ago. It was a highly competitive pitch for a really big account, that had previously done some high-profile advertising. I allocated a great strategist on my team for the pitch, said I'd be there with advice if needed, and got on with my day job. Time-wipe a few days, and the fabulous person had been dragged away on some other emergency. With a heavy heart, I stuck that particular monkey on my back (actually, I think it's called 'leading from the front') and said I would do the pitch myself.

I was convinced I would need to fake interest (in as sincere a way as possible) and also, to bite my tongue that training to kill was not a nice thing to do. Anyway, I duly started on my familiarization journey, met the brigadier in charge and went on a series of visits to training camps, to live military exercises on Salisbury Plain and to Sandhurst. I also interviewed a wide range of parents, teachers and current and potential recruits of all stages and backgrounds about why the Army might be an appealing thing to do.

The thing that most affected me was visiting the early-stage Army training centre, where a lot of spotty and sulky 16- and 17-year-olds went in at one end, and emerged seven weeks later transformed. Not into the bloodthirsty warmongers of my prejudice, but into young men who had found close friendships and often substitute families amongst their platoon colleagues and commanding offic-ers. They had developed a sense of purpose and confidence, their shoulders were a bit further back, and they had learned practical skills like driving and fixing machinery (as well as shooting things).

What they wanted above all was to make the best of themselves. Some felt a strong sense of responsibility that 'someone had to do this tough stuff' of protecting freedom and democracy from those who would squash it by force, and they felt they could do it well. Others had more basic motivations, and felt that, of the job options available, this one might give them more practical skills and help their future employment prospects. Most found a whole lot more.

What's more, I discovered that the British Army was genuinely considered one of the best, if not the best, professional army in the world, and trained all kinds of world leaders, which often generated lasting comradeship and goodwill. The British Army is a truly soft 'hard power' for the UK.

Out of all this background came the 'Be the Best' campaign line, which is still running to this day. I'm not sure whether a 'Be Nice' line would exactly fit the bill in the same way, but I found nice guys and decency in unexpected places.

They also weren't finishing last.

Being good is good

Aside from the high-profile business villains, there are many more mediocre leaders who are doing an acceptable job, and getting away with it. And whilst they're not clubbing baby seals, they're not contributing to the sum of human happiness either.

This might feel a bit depressing on the 'good guys' front (and as an aside, it would be good to find a better term other than 'guys' for this kind of informal collective noun for a group of men and women; maybe just 'people' would be good?) But on the upside, there is growing evidence that 'nice' and happy businesses perform better.

A few examples. Havas Media's Meaningful Brands Global Study showed that purpose-driven, more 'meaningful' brands outperformed the stock market by 134 per cent in 2019. Research by EY and *Harvard Business Review* showed that the revenue of purpose-driven businesses grew 10 per cent more than the flatline of the businesses that lacked the soul stuff.[1] And Unilever, one of the world's biggest and most successful consumer goods businesses, reported that its purpose-driven brands are growing at twice the speed of the others.

I haven't got an X-ray machine to peer inside the former Unilever CEO Paul Polman's heart, but from what I can glean, he has some strong views on purpose, decency and the central importance of sustainability in business, in all its meanings.

Nice business is good business indeed.

SO, WHAT DO I MEAN BY NICE?

Well, how about someone who:

- builds confidence in others, listens and encourages;
- runs a business as a human enterprise (with balanced metrics like customer, employee, social and environmental measures as well as profitable outcomes);
- wants to do the best for customers (versus the least they can get away with);
- doesn't abuse power, but uses it to do more good;
- is honest when they make mistakes and goes beyond the call of legal duty to put it right;
- takes difficult decisions, but is humane and helpful at preparing people for another job;

- recognizes toxic people and if they can't be healed, asks them to leave a business, no matter how many sales they bring in;

- is curious and open-minded about new ways of working and getting stuff done;

- sees the future coming and adapts the business in a timely and appropriate way;

- recognizes that if you don't make sure that society more broadly understands and benefits from what you do, business won't be seen to work for them;

- is nice to animals and life on earth as well as humans.

Not that much to ask, really.

At the extreme end, nasty leaders are a risk. Their people are scared, so bad decisions go unchallenged, or talent leaves, or frankly the rest of the organization ceases to care and just takes the pay cheque whilst secretly undermining the business. On this, research suggests that companies with 'engaged' employees deliver an operating profit up 19 per cent. Those with disengaged staff have profits correspondingly down by 24 per cent.[2]

I vividly recall when the CEO of an organization I worked with said that, if the staff didn't think that the finance director was a complete bastard (I'm afraid he used a worse word than 'bastard', but I will gloss over that for the moment), then you'd got the wrong person in the job. And this finance guy duly proceeded to bully the poor young executives about minutiae on their expenses, whilst ensuring that the senior team got huge bonuses.

This is the stuff that lies behind revolutions, as we know.

When Jane Shepherdson, former CEO of Topshop (part of the Arcadia Group) was asked about her experiences of working with Sir Philip Green, she didn't hold back:

> There is no question he was a bully. Everybody knows he was a bully.
>
> He did bully people but he didn't bully me. He tried to – he would get very angry and shout a lot, and I would then get very angry and shout a lot. I wasn't properly angry, I just knew the way to talk to a bully was to pretend to get very angry, to shout at them and then every time I did that he would back down.
>
> It was really exhausting doing it. It takes its toll on you. You have to constantly be making yourself aggressive.[3]

Losing quality, talented staff and terrifying the others is guaranteed to damage the business. It also gives the business a bad smell for investors as well as future recruits. It's a vicious circle.

Just one of Arcadia's legal bill estimates in 2019 was £3 million.[4] Just think of what else the business could do with all that money and better-placed energy.

There's enough misery around, and the world can be a difficult enough place as it is, without people being unpleasant to each other. In fact, it's imperative on us all to make every human interaction as positive as it can be.

People can scoff at 'do good' campaigns like 'pay it forward', and people such as Ellen DeGeneres and Oprah Winfrey having a few million dollars to pay away. But on a simpler, more recent note, Oprah also said, 'You've got to lean to the happiness.'

Could someone make her President please?

THE TROUBLE WITH BULLIES

Fortunately, it's easier to deal with bullies these days. Companies know that bullying is an expensive word because of the hard cost of legal and reputational risk, and the loss of talented people, so complaints get listened to.

If you feel someone is bullying you, start with talking to them and trying to give them the benefit of the doubt: 'I am sure you did not mean to come across as this, but this is how it made me feel, so please approach it differently next time'. If it happens again, re-state your feelings and put it in writing. Involve the HR team.

In my experience, bullies are often taken back if you push back.

Remember, it's their problem, not yours. But you can manage how you deal with it with the help of colleagues or HR if you need it. And, of course, if you get to run the organization, you can eject all the bullies you want.

In the pre-Trump, pre-Putin-power, pre-'throw your weight around and see what you can get' politicians, several governments were serious about having a 'happiness and well-being' index as a measurement for the success of their societies. After all, what are we here for than to try to make the world a better place? This happiness stuff has been drowned out for the moment.

Thinking further about the constant 'stick' rather than 'carrot' way of managing, if you're not nice to people at work, particularly more junior people, you can bet your bottom dollar that the person you may have ignored or patronized along the way is going to end up being able to give you business or help you at some point. And as a

NICE GUYS DON'T FINISH LAST

result of your un-niceness, they may, their own niceness aside, take some guilty pleasure in not doing so.

People who are rude to waiters, cleaners, service staff or anyone junior to them whilst creeping up to their bosses and peers really give me the creeps in turn.

The number of times I've had a smiley person the other side of the table who turns dismissive when the waiter shows up. These people plummet in my estimation.

So, I think it's good to be, and be known for being, nice.

Not nice

Nice obviously doesn't have to mean nicey-nice in a door-mat, pushover kind of way, where people feel they can rip you off, do bad work or generally take advantage. Being nice is sometimes giving people difficult feedback because they need it to get better – and indeed, for them to be nicer from time to time themselves.

Not just because it works better. Even if the 'hard' evidence weren't there, again, it's just better (and nicer) for everyone.

This is never more the case than when you're choosing a life partner. In fact, friends and partners in general.

I know too many women who are intelligent, attractive, vital, full of potential. But, for whatever reason, they have ended up with people who reduce them.

If ever I share the equivalent of my Ten Top Tips, then once I've gone through the usual suspects like the impor-tance of presentation, skills, experiences, getting yourself organized, etc, at tip No 10 I will usually say, 'Only have a relationship with people who make you feel good about yourself.' This goes for friends as well as lovers and partners. And it doesn't mean it has to be someone who always (and only) tells you the good news – it's just that their motivation needs to be positive, supporting you to be as good, happy and successful as can be.

There was a poignant example of this in a company I was involved with. A really attractive, vivacious and bright woman, who at one time was viewed as a high-potential manager with the confidence and manner that reflected that. Roll forward a few years and her features and bearing had changed. She had developed a nervous laugh and her face showed traces of sleep deprivation and strain. I gathered she had an 'on–off' boyfriend; he was unreliable in the fidelity department, but would always come back. Because, frankly, why wouldn't he when she always took him back, earned a decent living and looked great? Anyway, they eventually got married and had a baby. Then another. She still managed to hold it together but again, bad stuff showed, in her face, body and eventually her work.

I am not one to criticize how anyone else looks when they are either pregnant or generally being a mother, but this was different. In addition to the usual round of sleep problems, work stress and guilt, she had the extra burden of a critic and viper as a partner in the nest. She later mentioned that he even criticized how she cooked for her children. Life was one long abrasion.

What was it about her that she somehow felt not worthy of a decent partner, that she would prefer to have someone who 'treated her mean'?

Anyway, I later gathered that she finally split and settled into a steady career as she tried to manage life as a single mother. I am sure, though, a big part of her was relieved and liberated.

I also recall another friend, who used to say to me, with a sigh, 'You know, you really married well. I didn't'. She didn't mean that I had married a rich guy, or one with obvious prospects at the time (because that certainly wasn't obvious). Just someone who has been really supportive, believes in equality and feminism without a hugely self-conscious effort. In contrast, the guy she married was, again, someone to be managed, humoured and trodden around as though on eggshells.

Exhausting, and particularly when you have a demanding job already, let alone looking after children together. (NB: whenever I hear someone talk about having a baby 'to bring them together with their partner', I have to organize my features into a calm carapace, whilst I am thinking catastrophic thoughts.)

Hiring and firing

I've been incredibly lucky in the 'other half' department and am careful not to take it for granted. Being a classicist means that I know hubris is followed by nemesis. Whenever I say to people that I'm lucky, that I have a very supportive partner and that we have somehow managed to feel like we have made more of ourselves together than we would have done separately, I am inwardly steeling myself not to tempt fate. But perhaps again this is the imposter syndrome at work.

But, honestly, in terms of blurring work and personal life in a useful way – if you're good at, or can get good at, recruitment at work, you can hopefully get good at 'nice' partner recruitment too.

It's easier these days, because the 'trying people on' pyramid is inverted. In the old days, if you weren't fortunate enough to get to know people well enough (ie to really know them) from school, university or work (and to know that you had things in common or they weren't a psychopath), you might meet someone at a party, in a bar or club. You might have chemistry (even explosive) but discover over the next few months or even years that you have little else in common. And without putting too fine a point on that, chemical reactions eventually go flat. Today, in the personal equivalent of LinkedIn, you have the opportunity to 'recruit' a potential partner (through the better online dating sites) who has similar interests and values to you – it's then just a small matter of meeting enough people until you find someone that you have chemistry with too. Treating it like a hobby, and meeting two people a week for a year can be called 'test and learn'. That's personal business.

In case this is beginning to feel like I am more familiar with dating sites than is appropriate for a happily married mother of two, I should just emphasize that I have got this experience by vicarious means. Mostly from busy executive women friends who have found love – and had a family in some cases – with spooky efficiency and effectiveness when they were too busy to let it be random.

Having a supportive partner is a helpful ingredient in life, and can contribute a lot to success and happiness. And so it's worth investing a 'professional' level of time and effort in. But if you're happier living alone, then more power to your elbow. That's the other 'nice' thing about life now. You can have support systems to do what you wish, with or without someone sleeping with you.

As seen on screen

As a slight health warning, even if you're trying to be 'nice', by sharing your experiences in case they're helpful to others, it can be fraught with difficulties and sensitivities – so much so that you wonder why on earth you put yourself in harm's way.

I was asked to appear on a TV programme when my children were small, and as I really liked and trusted the producers I met, I agreed. They wanted to feature a spectrum of motherhood in the programme, and that would mean I would be representing the full-on working mother end. Perhaps you can see where this is going – all I would say in my defence was that I felt it was a bit of a duty to try and represent business women and working mothers in as positive a way as possible.

As I was also representing the business angle, they wanted some footage of me driving home from work in my company car, talking to our nanny on the car phone whilst she was looking after the children and anticipating my arrival. It was actually a reasonably balanced programme, and it wasn't as though they made up the fact that I often called my nanny on the car phone on my way home. My daughters actually looked quite happy and healthy in the programme and even managed to look pleased to see me when I got home. It didn't stop people commenting about how they felt I was being a rubbish mother not being at home with the children and checking in by phone. As an aside, my now husband/then partner was sensibly having none of it, and the producers were reduced to showing a photograph of him holding one of the children, with me saying what a supportive partner he was – although clearly not supportive enough to be there in the flesh.

Frankly, they didn't know the half of the 'Bad Mother' syndrome. You particularly know you may have done a slightly less than excellent job in managing your children's upbringing when they become teenagers. One of my daughters was staying at a friend's house when she was about 14. They were home alone for a while in the evening (I didn't know that this would be the case) and they thought they heard a noise downstairs. They were worried this might be someone breaking in, and were seriously thinking about calling the police. Although we live in the UK they were going to dial 911 rather than 999. Yes, that's the kind of agony you have to reflect on when you allow your children to watch too many American TV series in the name of peace and quiet. Ultimately, the noise was nothing, and they were fine. Phew.

And whilst we're at it, I'm not claiming that I have never, at any point, behaved in a difficult way at work. Whilst I have been told that I am usually calm and support- ive, I have without doubt shown the usual failings of tired- ness, stress, disappointment and normal life. If I didn't notice and didn't apologize appropriately at the time, then sorry. Truly.

I could have danced...

Before I sign off this chapter, it would be incomplete if I didn't share an early memory that brought home to me the difference that a nice-versus-nasty mindset can have.

When I was a little girl, I was in a dancing competition in London. I emphasize that, because in my hometown dancing school, people were, or usually feigned being, nice and supportive. But in the All-England competition, there was an 'All-England' level of competitiveness and psycho drama. In my group, I was competing against a few girls, and one of their friends came up to me just before I was due to go on stage.

She eyeballed me with admirable focus. 'Just remember', she said, 'my friend's gonna win, and you're gonna lose.' Clearly, she was showing a remarkable and precocious pre-NLP level of understanding of the concept before it was mainstream. In fact, her friend finished third, and I was one above her.

Nice girls don't finish last. Maybe second sometimes.

Honestly, you can kill with niceness and kindness. So, go and knock 'em dead.

NOTES TO SELF

- Don't believe macho garbage about niceness being weakness – that's not borne out by data, and nastiness is a BIG risk.
- Recruit nice people. In work, life and play. Particularly life.
- Just be nice, period. What goes around comes around.

CHAPTER ELEVEN

You and the future of business

On why the business world really needs... YOU. All of you, flaws and all

On the subject of saving the world from evil, I loved the film *Warm Bodies* with Nicholas Hoult and John Malkovich.

It's one of those films about young love that makes grown women feel all warm and wistful. I would put it in the same category as sneakily watching *all* the *Twilight* films (the first one was by far the best, in my view, although obviously I had to watch all of them to compare).

The main difference between *Twilight* and *Warm Bodies* is that, whereas Robert Pattinson/Edward Cullen is a vampire, Nicholas Hoult/R is... a zombie. The film is a zom-romcom.

Set in a post-apocalyptic world, there's a war between zombies (ex-humans) and surviving humans. One of the 'young' zombies (R, played by Hoult) kills a human girl's boyfriend, eats his brains (tough watching for me as a vegetarian), starts getting 'feelings' and then rescues the girl from the other zombies. It's better than it sounds.

Gradually, R starts to come back to life. His human heart revives and beats again. He also leads the reconciliation between the humans and the other zombies, who have also shown signs of (nice) humanity from watching the young couple fall in love. The only exceptions to this are scary things called 'Boneys', skeletal zombies who prey on anything with a heartbeat and have gone too far down the dead track to come back.

In the end, the humans and 'nice' zombies join forces and kill most of the Boneys, and human society is together again. Ah, it's nice.

I would be lying to say that I took a profound message from the film at the time but there was the usual sense of satisfaction when the doubters are converted, the baddies are squashed, and love conquers all to make the world a better place.

Changing the chemical balance

Building on the obvious allegory, it would be nice to get enough good human beings into positions of influence and power so they can convert any willing business zombies (even those secret ones), and escort those beyond hope to a secure care facility.

And yes, I hope this means YOU. As a good human being.

I have listened to lots of heated conversations over time about how 'people' need to do x and y to fix the world, about how 'people' need to make it fairer, to depose the wrong people who are in charge. But again, I am hoping that YOU are 'the people' to do that.

I've covered this in previous chapters, but I'll say it again here. I'd like to see many more women running organizations – as so many of us would. The world needs a different hormonal and chemical balance at the top of all institutions. And I don't just mean being senior, I mean being Chair, CEO, MD, Director General, President. The person calling the final shots, mixing it with all the other people who call the shots and impact the wider world. I'm aware that often that person 'at the top' doesn't feel completely in charge when they have shareholders, vast workforces and/or voters, but 'tone from the top' makes a big difference.

If you're capable of running an organization – and I think we can guarantee that there are a lot more women capable of doing this than think they are, or who have been given the chance to – then it's worth thinking about whether you feel it might even be a social responsibility to do so.

I have spoken to so many brilliant women who admit that, even if they were being considered, they have held back from leadership positions because, understandably, they feel it's a lot of hassle and angst, that it wouldn't fit with their lives, that they'd rather work for themselves or even freelance for a few years. It is difficult to disentangle how much of this is tied up with imposter-style self-doubt over a long period, but it's not difficult to see that if you judge yourself harshly and don't believe you'll get the right support, running an organization at the very top looks less inviting. And then it can often be difficult for women to get back into mainstream workplaces even if they wanted to. In parallel to the broader leadership discussion, it's really important to champion policies to ease this 'second coming', 'returnship' opportunity for women too.[1]

I know so many women in their 40s, 50s and 60s who would be more than capable of coming back into the corporate workplace if they chose, with all the skills they've learned about managing difficult people and situations (children, family, schools, builders), and about entrepreneurialism and self-employment, all of which, crucially, adds to their original workplace experience. And not just to do a middle-of-the-road job, but to ascend the company ladder. Some companies are doing some good things to encourage women back, but it should be the norm rather than the exception. Companies like Credit Suisse, Morgan Stanley, IBM, General Motors and several tech companies have interesting programmes, even if still on a small scale. More work needed by all.

Us against the world

Clearly, as an alternative route, women can create fabulous beacon businesses with interesting start-ups and sole trader enterprises. It's fantastic to see that the number of women-owned businesses increased nearly 3,000 per cent since 1972 in the United States according to the 2018 *State of Women-Owned Businesses* report.[2] Less good, though, is that in 2017, only 17 per cent of start-ups had a female founder.[3]

However, without putting too fine a point on it, there are too many sharp-suited people running big, influential businesses and institutions that have the power to puncture those nice beacon-business bubbles. And if we have divided communities, a degraded environment, and an unhappy workforce in wider society through leaders behaving badly, it's more difficult to feel great yourself.

Also, as we know, starting a business and working for yourself is not without stress – finding the next customer or piece of new business without resource or a high-profile brand name around you can be pretty challenging.

The good thing is that, these days, with all the public pressures on organizations to create diversity in general, and deeper awareness of things like unconscious bias, gender-neutral parental leave and so on, there is definitely a more open door for those interested in doing things differently. And a lot that anyone can do to get themselves in that position.

Because we so need it.

The world is up to you

Forgive the overkill mentions, but the theme running through this book, and specifically in this chapter, is that achieving this change needs you. Here are a couple of examples.

My sister doesn't mind me giving you a down-to-earth example from her working life. She is a bit older than me, and from a generation who were made to feel that jobs for women were less important because you were going to leave work to bring up your children. If you wanted to go back and do a bit of part-time afterwards, the reasoning went, then fine, but frankly, it wasn't going to amount to much.

When she did go back to work part-time at a pretty good company, she used to tell me how her managers were screwing things up, that they had little idea of how to motivate people and that, honestly, she felt like just doing the minimum to get by. Not particularly gently, I suggested to her that if she didn't like the way she was being managed, then why didn't she offer herself as a manager and do it the right way? She told me that, frankly, she didn't need the hassle of stepping into a management position. I told her that, frankly, she then needed to accept whatever manager the company threw her way. That's sisterly love for you.

If you want a better manager, that may need to be you.

I'm painfully aware that I think I probably walked away from the CEO role a bit too soon when the going got tough, and I didn't 'get going' in a good way at the time. I hated it. It's true that it was in extreme circumstances post-9/11 and at the time I couldn't see a way to do that particular CEO job long term in a way that I felt I could live with. I *think* (hope) that I might make a different decision now.

At least it helped me understand what a difficult and relentless job being CEO can be, so I can use this to help others. Being Chair has been great, although it's worth remembering that it's not your job to run the business any more and even if you hire a terrific CEO, you can find yourself biting your tongue off in a 'I-wouldn't-do-it-that-way' kind of way. As Chair, you can influence, cajole, challenge and sometimes fire the CEO if necessary, but in the end, you've got to shut up from time to time and let them get on with it. It can be a little frustrating.

There's a rather different example from someone who used to work with me. I am incredibly proud of what she has done, and she eventually became CEO of a major group. But when she originally joined that group as a department head, she confided to me that the company had an annoying and alienating macho culture. And whilst they seemed to rate her highly, and she felt that the company had potential, she also felt patronized and was thinking about moving on. Sadly, I can't take much credit for what happened next – maybe because I secretly wanted her to return to working with me.

Having got some decent professional coaching (of the 'why *can't* you do that/ask that' kind), her personal revelation was that, if she didn't like something, she had two choices. Either, she could run away to another company in a similar senior, but still not 'in charge' role, and take the risk that the grass might not be greener. Or, she could position herself where she could *get* in charge. In fact, her company was looking to hire a new MD, but I gather hadn't considered her for the role because she was a strategy specialist and, as a woman, was 'probably happier in the supporting role'. I use inverted commas here because of the number of times I have witnessed men discussing senior management succession and not seeing the potential of the female talent in front of their noses because they don't look and sound the usual part.

With a bit of bolstering and scripting by her coach, this fabulous woman stared down the company's owners, and said that she wanted to do the MD role, that if she left, there was obviously a danger that clients would take their business away… and that all she needed to do the job was their support and confidence. She duly got it and even managed to negotiate a decent package with some help from her (female) coach. She is now running a big group of companies, has promoted lots of women to senior roles, and has some of the highest levels of employee satisfaction in the industry. She has had some children along the way, and just told the shareholders how she would be organizing her working week to take that into account.

That's the power of being in charge.

It helped that she had leverage with the client relationships, and also that she had shown some commercial and general management capability in her previous role. You can't just say that you fancy the MD role if you can't assemble a decent business case for the chance.

It's tempting to burst in symbolically with some 'be the change you want to see in the world' quotes and to take a leaf from Beyoncé's song book about girls running the world in a military leather two-piece.

Except we don't.

Run the world.

There are fantasy pop songs, and then there's real life.

It's easy to get depressed about a world in which some nasty, greedy people give market economies a bad name, where big and small bullies seem to 'win', and where people fear difference and seek to keep apart.

But it's also a world where so many want things to be better, for the world to be more human (and which also looks after things that are not human but important to the world), where people live and work together for positive ends, and where the bad guys are converted or fade away. A bit like the *Warm Bodies* film in fact.

The truth about cats and dogs

In 1993, former BBC news presenter Sir Martyn Lewis supposedly claimed that television should feature more 'good news'. This was over and above the much-lampooned '…And Finally' quirky stories at the end of news broadcasts, where you can hear and feel the presenters crunching through the gears going from famine/people in peril/financial scandals/crashes to a lighter 'fun' tone. At the time, Lewis was eviscerated by the 'sophisticated' commentariat for allegedly saying something so crass as to want to talk about anything other than human and planetary misery.

As an aside, shortly before that, he had published a cute and funny book about *Cats in the News* (followed a year later by, yes, *Dogs in the News*).

Again, much mirth and disdain amongst the 'serious' and hard-bitten newshounds about the relevance of cats and dogs.

Now, 25 years later, as a bit of 'revenge of the nice guy', what are the most popular and viewed video phenomena on the internet? BuzzFeed's Jack Shepherd recently described the internet as a 'virtual cat park', at a time when there were more than 2 million cat videos on YouTube, with an average of 12,000 views each. Just in 2015, an exhibition called 'How Cats Took Over the Internet' opened at the Museum of the Moving Image in New York. It's apparently dogs' turns next.

We may have reached and passed 'peak cat', but perhaps it's indicative of something about good people being able to see things about the world that others can't or won't. I think it may bode well for the salvation of the human species at some point.

Bigging things up

One of the many-to-infinity issues around having so-called 'strong men' in charge of so many countries is that, no matter how much disapproval people express about aggressive behaviour, there is a sneaking suspicion that, if you want to get your own way in this world, that is how to get it. People may secretly feel glad they've got the school bully on their side in a difficult world.

In his iconic book from 1989, *Liar's Poker*, Michael Lewis coined the phrase 'big swinging dicks'. It's used to describe those (men) who became the most revered in the world of late '80s finance. I am sure that all those leaders, who still see this metaphor as role-modelling, will feel very satisfied that they have 'won' as they sit in their post-nuclear bunker. They will make a blind world if we're not careful. There is, of course, another way.

We need an equally powerful antidote. Adam Grant, the psychology professor from Wharton, writes in his book *Give and Take* about how 'givers' are more successful in the workplace.[4]

You don't have to be awful and make people scared and miserable to succeed. It's ironic that the world has become ultra-aware of bullying and harassment in certain quarters, and with a few organizational leaders getting hounded out or having to resign when exposed. But seemingly not with some political leaders. On a smaller and parochial level, just look at the House of Commons in the UK. Whilst we tell our children to be polite, be considerate and not yell at others, one glance at Prime Minister's Questions will tell them that actually, acting like an angry playpen when you're supposed to be responsible adults is acceptable.

If you are able to do it, please run a business. Get to the top and do it differently.

Whether we like it or not, business runs the world, so if we want to change the world, we need to change business, and how it's run. And by whom.

What do we make of all this?

There's just the small question of how.

So, here we are, feeling like imposters or otherwise. I've tried to pour as many examples and honest recollections into this book as I can remember or that I can bear to share. There may be some stuff buried deep down that refuses to show its face again.

I've tried to argue that the world needs some nice and applied hard drive if we're all to live and work in a place that we'd like. Or, frankly, just live in a world that hasn't been blown to smithereens. At the turn of this century, I remember reading cheery predictions from Lord Rees, at the time the Astronomer Royal, that he put the odds of humanity surviving until the end of the century at only 50/50.[5] Apart from potential natural disasters, this was in view of too many idiots being able to press the destruct button.

Your personal brand can save the world

I'm going to steal more brand thinking from the commercial sector that might helpfully be applied to your personal brand, to stimulate how you might go about world domination. And before anyone claims that branding has no place in what we're talking about, whether people like it or not, brands have the power to change the world – socially, emotionally and economically. Brands like Apple, Coca-Cola, or indeed WWF, have the power to cross boundaries and connect people in a way that governments never can. And when any brands behave badly, or become lazy and greedy, we all have the power to vote them out of our purchases and support in a heartbeat. Much more than can be said of governments.

These successful brands also generate long-term, reliable value and influence – if they live up to their promises. So, applying brand thinking to yourself can be one of the best ways of ensuring you get the most influence, and are as valued as you deserve, long term.

To reprise a few things that have cropped up through the book, there are three characteristics that have tended to make brands successful in any sphere, commercial or non-profit/charity. And, indeed, for personal branding. And those are: *clarity, coherence* and *leadership*. This always sounds so simple and easy, but as we know, simplicity can, ironically, be a bit complicated to achieve.

Try to apply these principles to Brand You for maximum effect.

Clarity

You don't need to be clear about the fact that you want to be President of the United States of America or CEO of Goldman Sachs at the age of six, but you do need to become clear about what drives you, what's important to you and what makes you happiest. Sometimes in your life you can be driven by the need to survive, the need to prove yourself to someone or something, sometimes to make a good living for you and the family, and, of course, sometimes because you can see a way of saving the world and all humanity.

COACHING FOR LIFE

When I tell people that I have got myself some coaching every few years for at least the last 20 years, they can look at me quizzically and occasionally pityingly (as in 'surely you must have got it together by now', 'why can't you just get on with it yourself?'). Funny how people don't say that stuff to athletes, who think it's normal to get coaching throughout their careers.

You might be pretty good at what you do, and I really enjoy coaching and mentoring other people, but it's very difficult to coach yourself. It's always a good idea to have an additional person to look at your performance and indeed life objectively, and figuratively speaking to spank your ass if need be. And if they're any good, they will be able to help you articulate and get clear what it is you do want and how to go about getting it – at least at certain stages of your life.

I was involved in a huge study in the late 1980s about the 'Yuppie' phenomenon. If you don't know about this, Yuppies were 'Young Upwardly Mobile Professionals' – watch the films *Wall Street* and *Working Girl* for some period pieces. This was an era of big shoulder pads, red braces and loud mouths, but it was also a time when there was a new and exploding breed of social mobility and opportunity in the West, unleashed by greater post-World War educational opportunities and huge white-collar job creation. This Yuppie study researched 20-something people to understand their motivations and aspirations. The opening sentence of the report was 'Yuppies are driven by fear of failure'. Well, at least that clearly explains why there was so much overt over-achievement – expressed in flashy money, clothes, apartments, cars, jobs and so on, as people were desperate to show they hadn't failed... Oh no, they were just SO successful. The clear drive was there, but not particularly directed to greater good.

A business friend of mine once explained why she had never got involved with a start-up enterprise. She felt a huge responsibility to look after and pay for all the other members of her family, including her parents and siblings. She had been by far the most successful one in business and financially and didn't want to put anything at risk. So, she accepted that she might be losing out on some entrepreneurial excitement and a big capital gain at some point in the future, but she was clear that she needed to keep on succeeding in a mainstream, reliable business, with a regular and substantial pay cheque. The skills she learned and how she presented herself reflected that clarity of need, even though she was, by nature, slightly quirky for the mainstream. By way of gesture, she called herself an 'intrepreneur' and spoke in an assertive and extrovert way, with outfits to match. But her business brain was so sharp, her humanity and humour out on her sleeve. All round, she was clear in what she needed, and made herself stand out in a sea of corporate greys.

These days, there's a much greater interest amongst both organizations and individuals in the importance of having a clear purpose behind your business and brand. In fact, you can hardly move for business and personal development books and articles on this subject. Even Justin Bieber called his 2015 album and world tour *Purpose*.

As far as I'm concerned, my range of purposes has gone from saving the world (when I developed that crush on David Attenborough at age seven), to getting enough money and status to feeling vaguely in control of my life, to keeping awake/conscious/functioning when my children were small, to trying to be a decent leader, then an expert practitioner in something, and now I seem to have got back to the future on wanting to save the world.

We need more 'saviour' brands – and people – to get it together to solve the urgent environmental and social challenges. And ideally to leave the world in better shape as a result of their activity, rather than just try to minimize impact. As the old saying goes, 'to live is to pollute'. Businesses need to do more to heal and enhance across boundaries, and are often in a better position than governments, who struggle to coordinate political agreement across national borders.

This re-charge of purpose reminds me of TS Eliot's *Four Quartets*, when he talks about how the end of our life exploration is when you arrive at your start point and really know the place for the first time. And sounds so much better than going round and round the houses.

Anyway, if you don't have some sense of clarity, anything else you do is likely to be less effective. And clarity in theory is one thing; making it show up coherently in reality is another.

Coherence

Once you know (even vaguely) what's important to you, and what you're about, make sure that shows up in your behaviour, acquired skills, personal presentation and the whole shebang as far as you can manage it.

If you want to be in the boardroom, if you want to influence shareholders, if you want to have the funds to make good investments, you need to be able to speak finance. I can't emphasize this enough, and in Chapters 4 and 5 I hope I made the case for financial knowledge. Practise a lot so you become fluent. If you can't get yourself on a course, you may even have friends who are accountants. I know I do, and I'm not afraid who knows it. Incidentally, apologies for this cheap and clichéd joke about accountants. I blame the classic British comedy *Monty Python*. If you're under a certain age, look it up. As you will know from earlier, I actually secretly wish I had got the accountancy qualifications. Buy your accountant friend a few drinks and get them to talk you through the basics, a few times over, and on practical examples like company Annual Report & Accounts. If it's not your natural habitat, treat it like a stretch as opposed to a comfort goal and practise some more. Practise saying it in an authoritative way. Don't forget that a lot of other people are making it up and making judgements too.

Equally, if you want to lead a creative business, for example (whilst still understanding what makes money or pays for people's jobs so you can feel vaguely in control), you need to symbolize your passion for the creative product, for people and performance – and, of course, it can be quite useful to look the part. Understand what's going on in the relevant creative scene, look as though you are fairly 'on it' from a style perspective. Perhaps channel your inner Vivienne Westwood if that's your thing. Deliberately decide whether to fully embrace or noticeably reject the symbols of the digital age, in line with their fit with your personal brand. For example, Burberry managed to combine traditional craftsmanship and digital innovation. Paperless Post does the same. Moleskine is determinedly about beautiful analogue books, albeit with one or two digital gestures.

As an example of how not to be coherent, I used to work with someone who headed a technology retail business. The company sold all the latest devices and consumer electronics. However, he used almost none of them. Although he talked about how interesting the new technology was in theory, his people picked up that he didn't have any personal experience or interest, and the rest of the business looked and felt ironically (and peculiarly) old-fashioned, with papers and physical files littering up the offices and tatty cardboard signs in the stores. He even used an old wired car phone when the rest of the world had moved to smartphones long ago. It might have looked post-ironic, quaint and retro to some, but to others it just said 'dinosaur'.

If you want to lead a company and the board, think about all aspects of both your skills (corporate governance experience? General management competence?) and also the vibes you are giving out in how you speak and how you present. To reflect what will reassure as well as interest people.

Although sometimes unpopular, Margaret Thatcher was a clear example of personal brand clarity and coherence in action, whether people liked what it did for her and the UK or not. She set out to be a strong leader, and that strength came to life though her deliberately re-trained and lower-toned voice, strong suits and handbags, iron-clad hair and, of course, her 'strong' – verging on unpalatable for some – policies and behaviour on campaigns like the Falklands War. Iron lady indeed.

I don't think you have to wear your 'iron' inside and outside all the time to succeed. If you're too brutal and people don't at least like you some of the time, then when things go wrong, expect that queue of people lining up to give you a good kicking. Out, in many cases.

Leadership

In any business or organization, it obviously matters who runs the show, and how they symbolize the best values of that business and its brand. This means making sure that the CEO cares and understands what the brand stands for, and its promise to customers and staff. I am sure I don't need to mention Steve Jobs, and how he symbolized the clarity of purpose, the human design, the efficiency and innovation of the Apple brand. He was beautifully clear, read obsessively, was vivid and efficient in how he expressed the Apple brand, and drove through design and innovation in keeping with the brand values – and was so consistent himself that he seemed to wear the same jumper and jeans for years. No twiddly, extraneous bits for him.

This contrasted with a rather different example of a CEO of the Coca-Cola Company back in 1999. After a product crisis in Europe (Belgium, in fact), Doug Ivester came out blinking from his office to meet the media storm, looking for all the world like a white middle-aged American accountant. Probably because he *was* a white, middle-aged American accountant. I didn't expect him to skateboard out of headquarters with a baseball cap on backwards, but it also didn't help that he seemed to exude a sense of 'corporate suit'. He didn't epitomize a modern leader for a contemporary global brand, let alone deal well with an international PR crisis.[6]

Leadership in branding for companies is also about restlessness, constant renewal, innovation, and setting the agenda. Those qualities are highly correlated with long-term value and influence in the commercial sector.

Of course, you're leader of your own personal brand. And that means you need to stay alert and keep yourself up to date with the world. If only people who say stuff like, 'Oh, my secretary prints off all my e-mails' could see themselves as others see them. I'm not suggesting you can't make a point of using a quill pen on parchment as part of your 'quirky' brand personality if that's appropriate, nor that you have to be on every social platform known to mankind (*sic*) and run the risk of looking like you're trying

desperately to be on-trend. You do, however, need to understand how the various social channels work – if only to
speak from personal experience about how ineffectual they
are and why you think they're doomed.

It's also important if you happen to be over 30 or indeed
the new 50 to over-compensate for the 'you don't get it'
syndrome for a new generation. Whilst you have every
right to challenge the business models, the effectiveness
and the absence of a long-term strategy in some 'new para-
digm' digitally born businesses, you've got to be really
careful that people don't just hear a crusty 'the old principles are the best ones, sonny' message.

Even if it's true.

And don't get into a lazy habit of only quoting old case
studies that give the game away. I still kick myself for once
citing an example from my previous British Airways brand
and advertising days. I was using the example of how BA
changed their visual identity in 1997 into diverse 'global'
tailfin designs, and then changed them back because some
Daily Telegraph readers didn't like them (and Margaret
Thatcher hated them too). For the record, I loved them,
and felt they symbolized an open-minded, global Britain.
Funny how these things come round... When I mentioned
this controversial PR battle at a mixed-level, multi-age
conference, at least 50 per cent of the audience had the
blank look that told me they had no idea what I was on
about.

You probably don't pay much attention to national
newspaper outrage when you're aged five.

I now try to have a mental equivalent of a swear box for
when I'm using older examples and historical stories.

My rule of thumb is that for every older example, I try to use two new and contemporary examples. It's a good discipline for forcing you to review and think new things anyway.

This is also a major part of keeping yourself constantly up to date in other ways. Skills, knowledge, doing new things. From understanding new corporate governance and global accounting standards (riveting, honestly), to visiting new growth markets in Asia and Africa, and doing courses on coding.

If you're at the younger end, 'leading' means to keep on growing your knowledge of different businesses, political and current affairs which may particularly affect you and your organization. Conquering any fear of public speaking (or becoming good at hiding it). You need to keep as much of yourself in the 'stretch zone' as opposed to the 'comfort zone' of personal development as possible, for as long as you can bear. But be careful not to venture too often into the 'no-go' zone and terrify yourself into retreat.

Which brings me on to the subject about regular renewal of how you present yourself. And yes, this can involve a fresh view of hair, make-up and clothes on a regular basis. Apart from the well-documented positive psychological impact these things can have on you personally, it does help to signal currency and care to those you might be seeking to influence.

And please don't read into this that women need to wear smart dark suits, rigidly coiffed hair and structured handbags. Absolutely not (and I only ever managed to score one out of three of these at any one point anyway). But it's a good idea to look and feel as though you have got your act (or at least part of it) together – to yourself and others.

This is not just a 'soft' female thing. Sir Clive Woodward, the much-admired coach of England's men's rugby team when it was at its most successful, believed very strongly that, if they wanted to be a world-class team, they needed to look 'world-class'. That meant stylish and state-of-the-art kit, training technology and changing rooms fit for champions. It all gave them confidence and helped them believe they were the best.

I sometimes idly worry if my hair and make-up freezes in time. But honestly, sometimes you've got to prioritize what you can physically and mentally get done in 24/7 without driving yourself mad. I find updating clothes easier and actually enjoy fashion – although when yet another '80s revival comes along, I always swear that if I wore it the first time round, I'm not wearing it again. Even ironically. People might think I meant it. Thus, I will now remain a stranger to padded shoulders in perpetuity.

I once had someone come round to my house to help me clear up and clear out my bulging wardrobes which I had been hoarding for years. This 'decluttering' woman was around before Marie Kondo became famous, and was fabulous with a tough-but-fair attitude that was very helpful. She held up every single article I had, asking things such as 'when was the last time you wore this? Do you love it and/or does it make you feel good?' If not, you stick it in one of a few piles: keep it for posterity; alter or clean it so you do like it; sell it or take it to a charity shop. She then put all my remaining clothes back neatly in my wardrobe, all colour coordinated. It's cleansing and satisfying, and makes going to work the next day feel like having a new and organized pencil case in time for school. So, keeping up with what's going on, and at any stage.

And in the end...

Above all, it's good to try and lead yourself and lead others in a way that befits a competent, confident and purposeful human being.

Yes, with all the messy emotions, insecurities and errors that we humans make.

Because that's what defines us as human, which can lead to greater empathy and greater, more positive motivation – and we all need the best versions of that at the top of the world. And everywhere else, really.

So, there we have it.

Hopefully, doing our bit to make the most of ourselves.

Hopefully, warm-hearted, warm-blooded, committed human beings, running warmer, more humane organizations, helping make the world work better for all.

Maybe feeling a bit naked sometimes, perhaps never quite feeling fully prepared.

Just you, all of us, and our friendly imposters.

Epilogue
Back to real life...

I make my way up some stairs to the sound of pounding music. I am dressed but the music's not the only thing that's pounding. My heart's about to burst through my chest.

I wait behind a screen whilst listening to the unmistakable sound of Beyoncé's Crazy in Love, *accompanied by the equally unmistakable sound of a lot of people talking and laughing. Oh shit...*

I am joined by a group of fit young women in the white vests and denim shorts of the original Beyoncé video, who 'collect' me from hiding. Through the fear, I at least feel relieved that I decided to go for the long track pants, bomber jacket and pulled-down cap – Bey's alternative look, minus the bubble gum.

Still, this was SUCH a mad idea.

I burst on to the dancefloor with the troupe of gorgeous girls, trying my best Beyoncé strut, and everyone's staring, probably in total shock. A lot of the people I love, or have loved or known well in my life have their chins dangling on their chest. My daughters' eyes have practically popped out. I almost trip up in remorse.

And then, thank goodness, a roar of recognition and some encouraging screeching.

I look around.

Just me, my family and friends.

And Beyoncé.

And I'm not dreaming…

OK, so I did have a naked midriff, but having (real) flu the week before had been quite useful in losing those last few pesky pounds (and a friend kindly sneaked a flattering photo that in the nightclub light made me look as though I almost had a 60-year-old six pack).

It was my party, and I cried and flash-danced as I wanted to.

I stole the thought of doing 'something' from an American friend who played in a band and serenaded his long-suffering wife at his Significant Birthday party.

I had even prepared. A couple of sessions with the very nice choreographer of the 'Hire a Dancer' company and ta-da! I had a few moves that bore a passing resemblance to the Bey video (in my dreams).

More than that, leading up to the Big Event (ie my Big Birthday), I joined a US-based online dance class to get in shape and remind my body (if not my mind) that I had wanted to be a dancer early in my life, that I loved doing it, and that I had really missed it while life/work/family/general slovenliness had intervened. Doing something that makes you happy, and renews you in some different way is also, yes, good for keeping your personal brand moving and grooving.

By coincidence, the fabulous founder of that online dance class (www.shinedancefitness.com) sent a note a few months later, saying that it was now possible to train and qualify as a SH!NE dance fitness instructor online.

So, well, I did just that in early 2019. I was ridiculously chuffed to get my certificate.

Funnily enough, my mum always wanted me to have a dance school. No matter what my dad thought, no matter my academic and work achievements, she always kept on about the fact that she thought I should have a dance school at some point. Funny how the circle of life works.

We'll see if I ever manage to do anything with that thought before I shuffle off this mortal coil.

Meanwhile, have a fabulous life, and I hope we might all dance, sing, love, and run companies together at some point. And hopefully save the world too.

The end

Acknowledgements

As this book is a collection of quite a few years of life and work experiences, it's quite difficult to assemble a manageable list of all the people who have contributed, consciously or otherwise, to everything I've been able to do – and everything I've written about in the book. I am sincerely thankful for all the support, advice, challenge, and the range of emotions and practical experiences bestowed.

As far as the actual book is concerned, I am incredibly grateful to the peerless Caroline Michel of Peters Fraser + Dunlop for her encouragement and advice in a much more personal book for me to write. Also, to the wonderfully thoughtful, empathetic and efficient Elen Lewis for taming my original (and rather more profane) sprawling draft and adding lots of great references and research. At Kogan Page, it has been great to deal with Helen Kogan and her team, and Chris Cudmore has been an exemplary Publishing Director – a combination of insightful, practical, tactful and clear in what he felt needed to be done to get the book into shape. He gently but firmly suggested that some of the more, er, 'informal' and confessional language (for which read rude words and asides) should probably be left to private conversations. Perhaps I'll get round to doing a Director's Cut one day for a bit of exorcism... On a serious note, many thanks to the publishing team.

There are so many people to acknowledge, both alive and some long dead, who have implanted bits in me and been role models – whether they were aware of doing it or not. For example, Mrs Legge at my junior school who saw some early academic potential and encouraged to me to help other boys and girls; the fearsome but kind Mrs Powell, deputy head at Wycombe High School, who took me under her academic wing after my father died and made me feel I could get into Cambridge (even if I wasn't classic material). My flamboyant and glamorous dance teacher Jeannine Greville, who was ambitious to get us all on to the stage and screen and made me a student dance teacher. The indomitable Joyce Reynolds who was my director of studies at Cambridge, and sent me those pointed but helpful handwritten notes over the years.

Then a whole torrent of people: Ann Murray of DMB&B, who taught me to work; Jennifer Laing, of Saatchi & Saatchi, who petrified me at the time; the late, great Patricia Mann of JWT, who was a board pioneer; the planners from whom I learned so much; Marilyn Baxter, who was one of my strongest professional influences and supporters – amazing brain, sense of humour and strength of character; the guys at Saatchi's (who will know who they are, and who made work fun as well as intense and ambitious); the head-hunter Isabel Bird, who believed that I could be a chief executive even when I didn't; my former colleagues at Interbrand, where I truly got to understand how powerful branding could be, and the fabulous team at BrandCap (soon to be re-christened) who continue to inspire me; the incredible Wendy Gordon, research guru, who taught me how to understand how people really think and behave; Dame Helen Alexander, who always had time for other female executives, and who died tragically young; all the amazing WACL women, who are so genuinely supportive; the coach and executive Catherine Baxendale, who (nicely) whipped my working life into shape to make time for the book; the friends and colleagues who read early drafts of the book and gave me honest feedback and suggestions; Patty Dimond, who helped make sure the financial bits were up to scratch, and Paul Harrison for his advice; Marksteen Adamson and the ASHA team, who have been generous and brilliant in helping me with my branding in general; Lorraine Ellison MBE, who has been relentlessly upbeat and cheerful in managing me; the superhuman (and very human) Debbie Klein, who I am proud to count as a friend; Lucy Aitkens of Sky, for all her help and perseverance. And, of course, my imposter.

But above all to my family, who keep me feeling loved and supported. They have truly helped me be my best self, flaws and all.

Notes

Prologue

1   Cocozza, P (2018) Night terrors: What do anxiety dreams
    mean? www.theguardian.com/lifeandstyle/2018/oct/03/
    night-terrors-what-do-anxiety-dreams-mean (archived at
    https://perma.cc/CXZ9-RLJG)
2   Cocozza, P (2018) Night terrors: What do anxiety dreams
    mean? www.theguardian.com/lifeandstyle/2018/oct/03/
    night-terrors-what-do-anxiety-dreams-mean (archived at
    https://perma.cc/2GBB-C3E8)

Introduction

1   Corkindale, G (2008) Overcoming imposter syndrome,
    Harvard Business Review, 7 May, hbr.org/2008/05/overcoming-
    imposter-syndrome (archived at https://perma.cc/TGY5-KHE9)
2   Sakulku, J (2011) The Imposter Phenonomen, *International
    Journal of Behavorial Sciences,* September, www.tci-thaijo.org/
    index.php/IJBS/article/view/521 (archived at https://perma.cc/
    XKC6-DL45)
3   BBC World News (2017) Women won't have equality for 100
    years, 2 November, www.bbc.co.uk/news/world-41844875
    (archived at https://perma.cc/VQ7E-BE8Z)
4   Zillman, C (2019) The Fortune 500 has more female CEOs
    than ever before, *Fortune*, 16 May, fortune.com/2019/05/16/
    fortune-500-female-ceos/ (archived at https://perma.cc/9GQZ-
    A34U)

5   Higginbottom, K (2018) Two-thirds of Women in UK suffer from imposter syndrome at work, *Forbes*, 29 July, https://www.forbes.com/sites/karenhigginbottom/2018/07/29/two-thirds-of-women-in-uk-suffer-from-imposter-syndrome-at-work/#2de4256e6ccf (archived at https://perma.cc/HE8T-BR26)

6   Dalton, S and Ghosal, S (2018) Self-confidence, overconfidence, and prenatal testosterone exposure: Evidence from the lab, *Frontiers in Behavioral Neuroscience*, 30 January, www.ncbi.nlm.nih.gov/pmc/articles/PMC5797613/ (archived at https://perma.cc/G99G-E8PY)

7   Edelman Intelligence (2019) Edelman Trust Barometer Survey, www.edelman.com/sites/g/files/aatuss191/files/2019-01/2019_Edelman_Trust_Barometer_Executive_Summary.pdf (archived at https://perma.cc/4P4P-8EAR)

8   World Inequality Lab (2018) *Trends in World Income Inequality*, The World Inequality Lab, wir2018.wid.world/part-2.html (archived at https://perma.cc/3F9B-Y78B)

9   Anderson, S and Pizzigatti, S (2018) No CEO should earn 1000 times more than a regular employee, *The Guardian*, 18 March, www.theguardian.com/business/2018/mar/18/america-ceo-worker-pay-gap-new-data-what-can-we-do (archived at https://perma.cc/W7ES-R8GJ) www.theguardian.com/business/2018/mar/18/amer (archived at https://perma.cc/T5S4-6XH9)

10 Hill, A and Giles, C (2016) Informed global elite places greater faith in institutions than majority, *Financial Times*, 17 January, https://www.ft.com/content/8f9ea1e2-bba5-11e5-bf7e-8a339b6f2164 (archived at https://perma.cc/T33R-REUG)

11 Windows 95 Launch, www.youtube.com/watch?v=lAkuJXGldrM (archived at https://perma.cc/EXC8-822M)

12 There is a vast body of research on the benefits of diversity and inclusion in the workplace. Catalyst collected some key findings in their 2018 report *Why diversity and inclusion matter*, www.catalyst.org/research/why-diversity-and-inclusion-matter/ (archived at https://perma.cc/QA32-ADV9)

13 Hunt, V, Prince, S, Dixon-Fryle, S and Yee, L (2018) *Delivering through diversity,* (McKinsey & Company, 2018). The authors measured profitability by average EBIT margin. www.mckinsey.com/business-functions/organization/our-insights/delivering-through-diversity (archived at https://perma.cc/BP88-EJ3Q)

14 Leon, GL (2005) Men and Women in Space, *Aviation, Space and Environmental Medicine,* 76(6), pp B84–88, Credit Suisse Research Study on gender diversity and corporate performance, www.ncbi.nlm.nih.gov/pubmed/15943200 (archived at https://perma.cc/W8RC-HKZE)

Chapter 1

1 For example, *Strong Fathers, Strong Daughters:10 secrets every father should know* is a 2007 parenting book by paediatrician, Dr Meg Meeker

2 Gladwell, M (2013) *David and Goliath: Underdogs, misfits and the art of battling giants,* Little Brown & Co

3 *The Guardian* (2017) University gender gap at record high as 30,000 more women accepted, Press Association, 28 August, www.theguardian.com/education/2017/aug/28/university-gender-gap-at-record-high-as-30000-more-women-accepted (archived at https://perma.cc/V49K-3HH5)

Chapter 2

1 Gray, C (2006) Stephen King, Obituary, www.theguardian.com/news/2006/mar/20/obituaries.readersobituaries (archived at https://perma.cc/A467-MM3H)

2 Spillane, M (2000) *Branding Yourself: How to look, sound and behave your way to success,* Pan Macmillan

3   Sakulku, J and Alexander, J (2011) The Impostor Phenomenon, *International Journal of Behavioral Science,* Behavioral Science Research Institute, 6(1), pp 75–97

Chapter 3

1   A Yale study led by LaFrance and commissioned by Procter & Gamble found that when subjects recalled a bad hair day, their self-esteem dropped. Specifically, 'bad hair' increased social insecurity and self-criticism and lowered performance self-esteem, hurting subjects' can-do attitude toward personal accomplishments, www.youbeauty.com/beauty/psychology-of-hair/ (archived at https://perma.cc/Z6FC-5ZCQ)
2   Gokalp, H (2016) Psychosocial aspects of hair loss, www.intechopen.com/books/hair-and-scalp-disorders/psychosocial-aspects-of-hair-loss (archived at https://perma.cc/AG3E-3UCA)
3   Moss, R (2017) Blonde Silicon Valley CEO dyes hair to be taken seriously, *Huffington Post*, www.huffingtonpost.co.uk/entry/blonde-silicon-valley-ceo-dyes-hair-to-be-taken-seriously-and-women-in-tech-are-not-surprised_uk_59b7abe0e4b027c149e21e89 (archived at https://perma.cc/VPN8-CKHG)

Chapter 4

1   Shankuntala, D (2006) *Book of Numbers*, Orient Paperbacks, New Delhi (from comment)
2   Busby, E (2018) Science degrees not appealing to girls despite rise in A-level take-up, *TES*, www.tes.com/news/science-degrees-not-appealing-girls-despite-rise-level-take (archived at https://perma.cc/AF6X-UW7D)

3 Stoet, G and Geary, DC (2018) The gender-equality paradox in science, technology, engineering, and mathematics education, journals.sagepub.com/doi/10.1177/0956797617741719 (archived at https://perma.cc/Y8KL-3LA3)

4 McKinsey & Company (2015) The power of parity: How advancing women's equality can add $12 trillion to global growth, *McKinsey Global Institute report*, www.mckinsey. com/~/media/McKinsey/Featured%20Insights/ Employment%20and%20Growth/How%20advancing%20 womens%20equality%20can%20add%2012%20trillion%20 to%20global%20growth/MGI%20Power%20of%20parity_ Full%20report_September%202015.ashx (archived at https:// perma.cc/5MTY-P7JQ)

5 Krivkovich, A, Nadeau, M-C, Robinson, K, Robinson, N, Stankova, I and Yee, L (2018) *Women in the Workplace Study 2018*, McKinsey & Company, www.mckinsey.com/featured-insights/gender-equality/women-in-the-workplace-2018 (archived at https://perma.cc/VHJ6-G37N)

6 Krivkovich, A, Nadeau, M-C, Robinson, K, Robinson, N, Stankova, I and Yee, L (2018) *Women in the Workplace Study 2018*, McKinsey & Company, www.mckinsey.com/featured-insights/gender-equality/women-in-the-workplace-2018 (archived at https://perma.cc/VHJ6-G37N)

7 Krivkovich, A, Nadeau, M-C, Robinson, K, Robinson, N, Stankova, I and Yee, L (2018) *Women in the Workplace Study 2018*, McKinsey & Company, www.mckinsey.com/featured-insights/gender-equality/women-in-the-workplace-2018 (archived at https://perma.cc/VHJ6-G37N)

8 Krivkovich, A, Nadeau, M-C, Robinson, K, Robinson, N, Stankova, I and Yee, L (2018) *Women in the Workplace Study 2018*, McKinsey & Company, www.mckinsey.com/featured-insights/gender-equality/women-in-the-workplace-2018 (archived at https://perma.cc/VHJ6-G37N)

9 Stevenson, J and Orr, E (nd) *What makes women CEOs different?* Korn Ferry, www.kornferry.com/institute/women-ceo-insights (archived at https://perma.cc/VD5Y-AEKD)

10 Zenger, J and Folkman, J (2012) Are women better leaders than men? *Harvard Business Review,* hbr.org/2012/03/a-study-in-leadership-women-do (archived at https://perma.cc/Q4X8-5PDM)

11 Noland, M, Moran, T and Kotschwar, B (2016) Is gender diversity profitable? Evidence from a global survey, Peterson Institute for International Economics, www.piie.com/publications/working-papers/gender-diversity-profitable-evidence-global-survey (archived at https://perma.cc/CY62-VX2L)

12 Nielsen Insights (2013) US women control the purse strings, www.nielsen.com/us/en/insights/article/2013/u-s-women-control-the-purse-strings/ (archived at https://perma.cc/EB7E-XHLR)

Chapter 6

1 Redfield, J (1994) *The Celestine Prophecy,* Bantam

2 The Landmark Forum, www.landmarkworldwide.com (archived at https://perma.cc/8TJB-WMC8)

3 Western, D (2020) Tony Robbins net worth, *Wealthy Gorilla,* wealthygorilla.com/tony-robbins-net-worth (archived at https://perma.cc/MXC3-L8LH)

4 Vernon, P (2017) Paul McKenna: 'I'm at the height of my powers', *The Times,* 14 January, www.thetimes.co.uk/article/paul-mckenna-im-at-the-height-of-my-powers-238wd6xlc (archived at https://perma.cc/U8TU-54UN)

5 Clifton, R and Maughan, E (2000) (eds) *The Future of Brands: Twenty-five visions,* New York University Press

6 Schein, EH (nd) Career Anchors Online, www.careeranchors-online.com/SCA/about.do?open=prod (archived at https://perma.cc/FD4G-SBG2)

Chapter 7

1   Institute of Directors (2013) Gerald Ratner speaking at the 1991 Institute of Directors Annual Conference, www.youtube. com/watch?v = Nj9BZz71yQE (archived at https://perma.cc/ QM4S-5FQW)

2   Mehrabian, A (nd) en.wikipedia.org/wiki/ Albert_Mehrabian (archived at https://perma.cc/9PQ4-5GP7)

3   Thomson, H (2014) Your voice betrays your personality in a split second, *New Scientist*, 14 March, www.newscientist.com/article/ dn25226-your-voice-betrays-your-personality-in-a-split-second/ (archived at https://perma.cc/F5GS-664A) and Klofstad, CA, Nowicki, S and Anderson, RC (2016) How voice pitch influences our choice of leaders, *American Scientist,* www.americanscientist. org/article/how-voice-pitch-influences-our-choice-of-leaders (archived at https://perma.cc/CYP3-GL5Q)

Chapter 8

1   Clifton, R and Maughan, E (2000) (eds) *The Future of Brands*, New York University Press

2   Ruello, O (2018) Jacinda Ardern: 'I'm not the first woman to work and have a baby', *Business Chicks*, businesschicks.com/ jacinda-arden/ (archived at https://perma.cc/55SB-KERJ)

Chapter 9

1   Egon Zehner (2018) Global Board Diversity Tracker: Who's really on board? www.egonzehnder.com/gbda (archived at https://perma.cc/58GP-HV3H)

2   Miller, CC, Quealy, K and Sanger-Katz, M (2018) The top jobs
     where women are outnumbered by men named John, *The New
     York Times* (unpublished Catalyst research and analysis)
3   Bureau of Labor Statistics (2019) Table 1: Employed and
     Experienced Unemployed Persons by Detailed Occupation,
     Sex, Race, and Hispanic or Latino Ethnicity, Annual Average
     2018, *Current Population Survey* (unpublished data)
4   Malhotra, S (2016) 50% Indian women drop out of the
     corporate employment pipeline between junior and mid-levels,
     Business Today, 5 October
5   British Business Bank (2019) Female start-up founders missing
     out on billions in funding, www.british-business-bank.co.uk/
     female-start-up-founders-missing-out-on-billions-in-funding/
     (archived at https://perma.cc/F9W4-PN6N)
6   Abouzahr, K (2018) Why women-owned start-ups are a better
     bet, *BCG*, www.bcg.com/en-gb/publications/2018/why-
     women-owned-startups-are-better-bet.aspx (archived at
     https://perma.cc/M69Y-DSZE)
7   Abouzahr, K (2018) Why women-owned start-ups are a better
     bet, *BCG*, www.bcg.com/en-gb/publications/2018/why-
     women-owned-startups-are-better-bet.aspx (archived at https://
     perma.cc/W6FA-WHM2)
8   Dowd, M (2018) Lady of the Rings: Jacinda rules, *New York
     Times,* 8 September, www.nytimes.com/2018/09/08/opinion/
     sunday/jacinda-ardern-new-zealand-prime-minister.html
     (archived at https://perma.cc/WPY6-5N94)
9   Roy, EA (2018) Jacinda Ardern on life as a leader, Trump and
     selfies in the lingerie department, *The Guardian,* 30 March,
     www.theguardian.com/world/2018/mar/30/jacinda-ardern-on-
     life-as-a-leader-trump-and-selfies-in-the-lingerie-department
     (archived at https://perma.cc/AAS3-H9F2)

10 Strack, J, Lopes, P, Esteves, F and Fernando-Berrocal, P (2017)_
Must we suffer to succeed? When anxiety boosts motivation
and performance, *Journal of Individual Differences,* 38(2) pp
113–24, econtent.hogrefe.com/doi/abs/10.1027/1614-0001/
a000228 (archived at https://perma.cc/373T-UX2H)

Chapter 10

1 *Harvard Business Review* (2015) The business case for
purpose, www.ey.com/Publication/vwLUAssets/ey-the-
business-case-for-purpose/$FILE/ey-the-business-case-for-
purpose.pdf (archived at https://perma.cc/52NV-JDW7)
2 Towers Perrin (2008) *Closing the engagement gap: A road map
for driving superior business performance,* Towers Perrin Global
Workforce Study 2007/8, www.eadion.com/site/uploads/Towers_
Perrin_Study.pdf (archived at https://perma.cc/DG78-8RVA)
3 Singh, A, Steafel, E, Barnes, S and Johnson, J (2018) Women
mean business, *Telegraph*, 21 October, www.telegraph.co.uk/
women/business/women-mean-business-can-close-gender-pay-
gap-follow-telegraphs/ (archived at https://perma.cc/PS52-6G77)
4 Sweney, M (2019) Philip Green faces £3 million legal bill as
new abuse allegations published, *The Guardian,* 8 February,
www.theguardian.com/business/2019/feb/08/philip-green-high-
court-action-against-telegraph-dropped (archived at https://
perma.cc/RN26-Q7XT)

Chapter 11

1 Mesure, S (2017) Women head back to work with 'returnships',
Financial Times, 21 February, www.ft.com/content/16ef6eb2-
9a8d-11e6-8f9b-70e3cabccfae (archived at https://perma.cc/
EQ9D-FGFY)

2   Castrillon, C (2019) Why more women are turning to
    entrepreneurship, *Forbes,* 4 February, https://www.forbes.com/
    sites/carolinecastrillon/2019/02/04/why-more-women-are-
    turning-to-entrepreneurship/#38fe6992542a (archived at https://
    perma.cc/9MS2-HBFR)

3   Teare, G (2017) In 2017 only 17% of startups have a female
    founder, *Techcrunch*, techcrunch.com/2017/04/19/in-2017-
    only-17-of-startups-have-a-female-founder/ (archived at
    https://perma.cc/H2L8-92H8)

4   Grant, A (2013) *Give and Take: Why helping others drives our
    success*, Penguin

5   Rees, M (2003) *Our Final Century?* Heinemann, www.
    telegraph.co.uk/culture/3594521/Our-odds-are-50-50-Our-
    Final-Century-by-Martin-Rees-228pp-William-Heinemann-
    1799-T-1599-plus-225-pandp-0870-1557222.html
    (archived at https://perma.cc/7TVB-WNXC)

6   Bennis, W and O'Toole, J (2000) Don't hire the wrong CEO,
    Harvard Business Review, hbr.org/2000/05/dont-hire-the-
    wrong-ceo (archived at https://perma.cc/3263-ED9M)

Index

NB: page numbers in *italic* indicate figures or tables

INDEX